THE
UNOFFICIAL,
ULTIMATE

TAYLOR
SWIFT

COCKTAIL
BOOK

RAS POUR

Photographs by Kelly Puleio

CLARKSON POTTER/PUBLISHERS * NEW YORK

CONT

Taylor Swift

FEARLESS

Speak Now

RED

1989

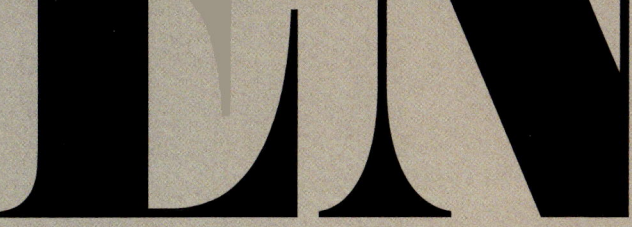

*Let's do this, are you ready? Let's f*ck shut up! Fuck it up up up up up!*

IT'S BEEN A LONG TIME COMING, SWIFTIES.

WELCOME TO THE UNOFFICIAL, ULTIMATE BOOK OF COCKTAILS INSPIRED BY ALL THINGS TAYLOR SWIFT!

At teatime, everybody agrees that T-Swift's rise from starry-eyed country starlet to full-blown global phenomenon is nothing short of enchanting. She's won more than three hundred major awards, including four Album of the Year awards at the Grammys, an honor that has yet to be surpassed by any other artist. She was the first woman to have more than one billion streams on Spotify. She has broken more than a hundred Guinness World Records, danced her way through the biggest-grossing tour of all time, and she's still going strong! It is impossible to summarize all her artistic and business accomplishments. In short, she is simply one of the greatest artists of our lifetime. An untouchable star, burning brighter than the sun.

In homage to her fearless genius, the following pages contain sixty recipes inspired by her life and art. Each chapter is dedicated to one of her famous eras—from her self-titled debut album in 2006 to *The Tortured Poets Department* in 2024—and features cocktails inspired by her greatest hits (with a few deep cuts tossed in for good measure).

There are laid-back sippers for stripped-down country ballads like "Tim McGraw," whimsical drinks for romantic moments like "Enchanted," cozy comforting ones for heartbreakers like "Back to December," and big, boozy heavy hitters for reputation-changing smashes like "Look What You Made Me Do." Of course, it wouldn't be good karma if this collection didn't include some recipes inspired by Taylor's favorite drinks, too. The Old Hickory Lake (page 33) nods to the time cooking queen Ina Garten introduced Tay to the whiskey sour in a Food Network interview in 2014. The Best Revenge (page 58) throws back to when she told *Vogue* her favorite cocktail was vodka and Diet Coke a few years later (time to tell the haters to take a hike!). Remember when the media heralded the return of the Cosmo in 2023 because she started to order the drink in bars in NYC? Or, when she set the internet on fire with recipes for the St-Germain-spiked French Blonde, perfect for a night out with the WAGs? These cocktails celebrate all those favorite moments in Taylor lore.

In the spirit of Tay's penchant for masterminding elaborate games and dropping Easter eggs in everything from song lyrics to her nail polish color, the savviest of fans will find little hidden surprises and references to her life and career sprinkled among the song names, ingredients lists, headnotes, and photos. For example, drinks like F*ck the Patriarchy reference her maple latte moment with Jake Gyllenhaal (you can keep the scarf at this point, JG), while Team Jacob hints at how the lyrics of "Back to December" (likely) reference Taylor Lautner. These are the obvious ones, but there will be even deeper references for the hard-core TS-sleuthers out there. (Also look out for the "From the Vault" callouts throughout for easy tips and suggestions for ingredient swaps.)

This collection of delicious drinks is for all of us—the Swifties, the Gaylors, the London Boys, and the Miss Americanas—to make a toast to the Queen of the music industry. Dip in to find a drink to pair with your favorite track when the mood strikes, raid it as a guide for pre-partying before her next tour, or use it to game out your next listening party. But before you dive in, check out the mixing tips and the pro intel on tools, glassware, and ingredients you'll need to make the drinks in this book. And don't skip the trivia—it's a hell of a time.

ARE YOU READY FOR IT? **1-2-3 LET'S GO, B*TCHES!**

YOUR (N/A) VERSION

(Alcohol-Optional Drinks)

Since we all know Taylor's Versions of her songs totally slay, and to make sure everyone at the party has a good time, twenty-one drinks in this collection can be made without alcohol—just look for **YOUR (N/A) VERSION** on recipes, which will explain how you can swap out the primary liquor for a nonalcoholic spirit. Thanks to the booming alcohol-free movement afoot these days, there are many top-notch options for boozeless "spirits" that run the gamut from gins and whiskies to rums, tequilas, and amari. Each recipe will include a specific recommendation for what to use in place of the traditional distillate, but you don't have to stick to those recs—half the fun is trying new options, so let your curiosity be your guide.

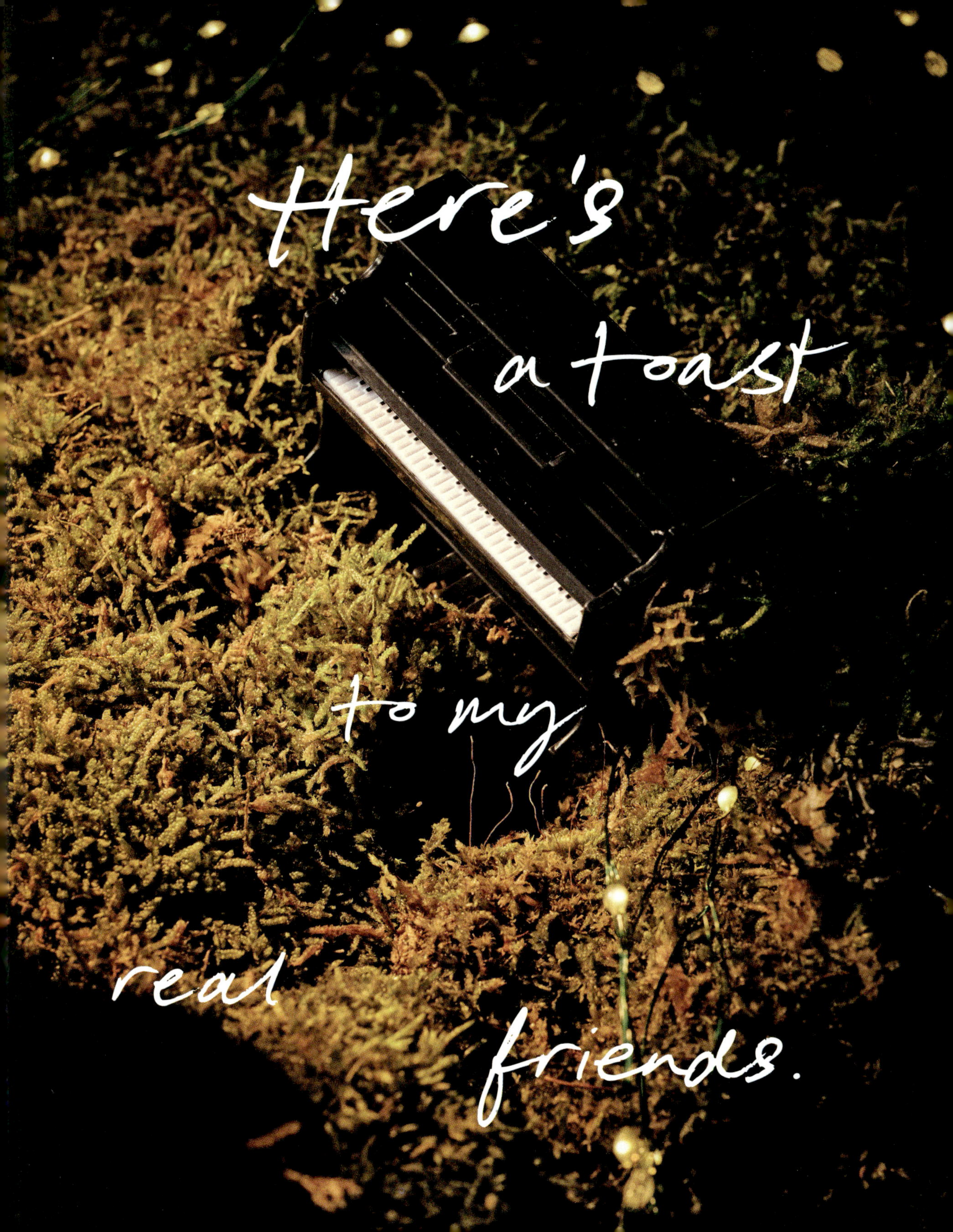
Here's
a toast
to my
real
friends.

MIXING
TIPS

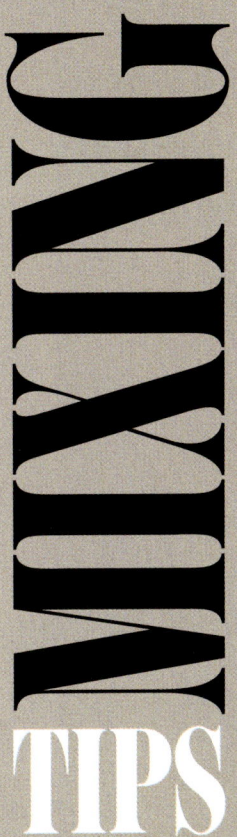

The recipes in this book range from super simple to slightly more complex. It doesn't matter if you're a casual drinker or a bona fide cocktail enthusiast, though—with these tips in mind, anyone can make a delicious round at home.

BE PRECISE WITH MEASUREMENTS

Mixing cocktails is like baking a loaf of bread or making cookies— the more precise you are with your measurements, the better the outcome. Always use a jigger to measure ingredients (see Tools for more intel, page 14), because the small hourglass-shaped tool has marks indicating common recipe measurements, whereas a regular measuring cup is usually too big, and teaspoons and tablespoons are too small (and require math for conversions). Could you free-pour your vodka and Diet Coke? Of course! But even in the case of a two-ingredient highball, knowing how much alcohol is going into the glass will be helpful in ensuring no one gets overserved. The more precisely you measure, the more control you have over how much you drink, and the better the cocktail will taste.

KNOW WHEN TO SHAKE (IT OFF) VERSUS WHEN TO STIR

If you learn just one thing about mixing drinks, make it this. Cocktails featuring citrus or dairy products need to be shaken to integrate those ingredients seamlessly. If you stir these, the texture will come out disjointed and the balance will taste off. However, cocktails made with only booze should be stirred, so they come out ice-cold and with a texture that's nice and silky.

KEEP THE SYRUPS IN PLAY

Nobody wants a drink that's too sweet, but syrups do more than just sweeten drinks—they are the glue that holds a cocktail's many components together in perfect harmony, ensuring the drink does not taste too tart or too astringent. That's why syrups are not suggested ingredients: They are a must! If you're nervous about having a drink that comes out too sweet, start mixing with less syrup than the recipe calls for, then taste the drink after you've shaken or stirred and add a bit more syrup in barspoon quantities until it reaches a nice, even balance. Think of this like "seasoning to taste," as cooks do in the kitchen.

ALWAYS STRAIN YOUR DRINKS

Use a strainer to filter your cocktail from the shaker or mixing glass into the vessel you're drinking out of. Straining keeps the ice you used to shake the drink—and unwanted bits and pieces from citrus or other fruits—out of your final cocktail. To do this like a pro, double-strain: Set a Hawthorne strainer over the mouth of the shaker tin and pour the cocktail through a fine-mesh strainer held over the glass. This is especially important for drinks that call for muddled fruit (like The Guy on the Chiefs, page 153, and Sequined Stars and Silhouettes, page 166), because nobody wants to chew on flabby pieces of peach or get blackberry seeds in their teeth while trying to enjoy a drink, right?

DON'T SKIP THE GARNISH

Garnishes serve a dual purpose: They make drinks look pretty, and they bring a pleasing aroma to the cocktail, which enhances the experience of drinking it. This is especially the case with fresh herbs and spices, but it applies to citrus, too. Whenever a citrus rind garnish is called for, squeeze the oils out of the peel over the top of the drink before you garnish—these aromatic oils help make the drink come alive. When you're cutting a peel from a citrus fruit, use a sharp paring knife or vegetable peeler and slice off an even strip of the top layer of the fruit's skin. You want the bright, aromatic outer layer (the zest) and not the white, spongy, sometimes astringent inner layer of the skin. The oils—and the flavor—live in the zest! When a recipe calls for a citrus twist, cut a long, thin spiral from the fruit using a channel knife, then wind it up in a tight coil with your hands before placing it on the edge of the glass as a nice visual flourish. If you cut the twist while holding the citrus over the top of the glass, some of its aromatic oils will land on the surface, enhancing the aromas at the same time.

EXTRA CREDIT

After you get the basics down, there are a few more simple things you can do to make drinks worthy of your wildest dreams. If you want to go above and beyond, take these tips into consideration.

KEEP IT FRESH WITH CITRUS

When picking out citrus fruit at the grocery store, give the fruit a little squeeze to make sure it'll be nice and juicy—if a lemon or lime feels rock-hard, chances are it won't have a good yield. Avoid wrinkled citrus fruits with blemishes—these are likely too old to have bright acidity. Lemons, limes, and grapefruits will stay fresh

for several days longer if stored in the refrigerator, but you will get more juice out of room-temperature citrus, so make sure the fruit has time to come up to room temperature before mixing drinks if juice yield matters to you. Always juice citrus as you are making a drink, to capture its most vibrant flavors; if you are making drinks for a party, you can squeeze a few hours ahead of time.

FORTIFY YOURSELF

Ingredients like vermouth, sherry, port, and other fortified wines like Lillet Blanc and Cocchi Americano (used in the French Blondie, page 165, and Forevermore, page 106, respectively) should be stored in the fridge to prevent spoilage. Style also matters—if a recipe like Sequined Stars and Silhouettes (page 166) calls for fino sherry, that is very different from amontillado or PX sherry, so stick to what is recommended for the best results. (For the record, fino is dry and bright with mineral notes, while amontillado tends to taste a bit nutty, and PX is lush and heavy like a sweet vermouth.) Similarly, not all vermouths are treated equally: Sweet vermouth is key for variations on drinks like a Negroni or a Manhattan, while dry vermouth softens the harsh edges of gin or vodka in martini riffs.

CHILL OUT

If you've been to a cocktail bar lately, you've probably seen ice in some fancy shapes. If you want to go top-shelf with your drinks at home, you can make ice cubes using a silicone mold (you can find many options online) and filtered water. The most useful size for making any kind of drink is the 1-inch-by-1-inch cube, but large single cubes and spheres are also a nice touch. Don't forget: The water used to make ice is important because it will influence the flavor of the cocktail as it melts. This goes for any ice you use (then discard) when chilling a cocktail in a shaker, and it goes double (or triple) for ice used for drinks served on the rocks or over crushed ice. Filtered water is best; use it when possible. Good ice is also a great upgrade because first impressions matter, and crystal-clear ice makes cocktails more beautiful.

DRINKS LOVE A FOREVER WINTER

Cocktails taste better when they are super cold! The glassware you use will influence this. Chill your glasses before mixing, and they'll keep the drink colder for longer. You can keep one set of your favorite glasses in the freezer all the time, so when thirst strikes, you're already set to grab one and mix, but if you don't have room for that, pop one into the freezer five minutes before making the drink—every minute helps!

TOOLS

Every good bartender has a well-stocked kit of bar tools, but you don't need a lot of fancy gear to make great cocktails. Just a few basics will do. Here are some recommendations for hitting all the marks with ease. In heels.

JIGGER

While jiggers have come in and out of fashion over the years, the measuring tool is a drink-maker's best friend, because precise measuring is the key to balanced cocktails. Every jigger is different, so finding one you like is personal—just be sure to get one that has clear measurement lines that you can see easily, so your pours hit the correct marks every time. The OXO brand has a few basic versions in the ballpark of $10 that get the job done.

SHAKER

Several options are available, but the shakers bartenders tend to use most are the two-piece stainless steel type, where a smaller tin fits into a larger tin. This "tin-on-tin" setup is best for getting drinks super cold, plus they're easier to open and close and more durable than glass. Basic versions can be found for $10 to $15. Koriko tins, the ones the pros use in the best cocktail bars, have weighted bottoms that help prevent tip-overs. They go for about $27 for a set—an investment well worth it if you make cocktails more than once a week.

FRUIT JUICER

When cocktail recipes call for citrus juice, it's always best to juice à la minute—buying commercial, shelf-stable juice will bring down the quality of your drink! You don't need a high-tech fancy juicer if you are not making drinks professionally (though props if you want to use one anyway). Instead, a simple hand-squeezing tool (in the $5 to $10 range) will be easy to use and easy to clean, too.

BARSPOON

Barspoons come in all shapes, sizes, designs, and finishes. Most important when you're choosing one is that the length, weight, and detailing of the handle all feel comfortable and proportionate to you when you hold the spoon. For beginners, a smooth handle might be easier to use than one with spiral indenting, which can take some practice to wield gracefully. Expect to pay about $10 for a good one.

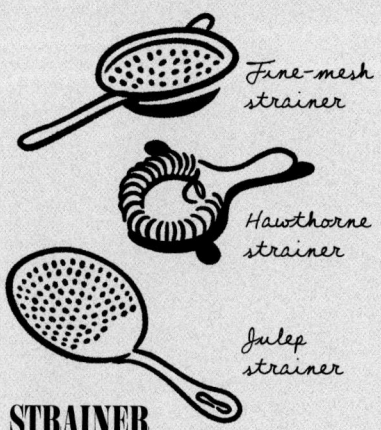

Fine-mesh strainer

Hawthorne strainer

Julep strainer

STRAINER

Shaken drinks always need to be strained, to keep ice and bits of citrus or herbs out of the cocktail. Many bartenders use a Hawthorne strainer—the kind with the metal coil on the end—and, when muddled fruits are involved, a fine-mesh strainer as well (this technique is called double-straining; see page 11). If you only make cocktails occasionally, a $5 Hawthorne strainer will do the trick, but if you like to entertain others and you make cocktails frequently, get a nicer Hawthorne with a good tight coil. For stirred drinks, you can use a julep strainer, which has larger holes and no coil, though you may be able to use a Hawthorne strainer if the size of the opening on the mixing glass fits the coils. You have options!

MIXING GLASS

Mixing glasses don't have to be fancy—you could use a shaker tin or a pint glass, if you want to—but the size is important. If you are typically only making one or two drinks at a time, a 19-ounce glass will suit your needs just fine. If you regularly entertain large groups, a larger 28-ounce version might be useful. Prices range from $10 to $30.

MUDDLER

A lot of drinks in this book call for smashing up fruit in the bottom of a mixing glass or tin before building the rest of the drink. This means you'll need a good muddler. These come in many sizes, finishes, and weights—your job is to find one that feels comfortable for you. Most are either plastic or wood and cost $5 to $10.

GLASSWARE

From a frothy sour in a pretty coupe to a tall cooler in a fancy Collins glass, cocktails just taste better when they are served out of the right vessel. Here are a few of the most common types you will need to make the drinks in this book.

COUPE, NICK & NORA, AND MARTINI GLASSES

For shaken or stirred drinks that are served "up"—without ice—these three cocktail glass styles are all classy options and can be used interchangeably. How to choose? Think about what aesthetic you want to bring to the drink—Nick and Noras have a vintage elegance, while coupes purr with Gatsby-era decadence. And there's nothing more iconic than drinking a gin martini out of a V-shaped martini glass. The other thing to consider is the surface area—Nick and Noras and coupes have a curved lip to cradle the liquid, while the wide-mouthed shape of a martini glass can make spills more likely. The smaller surface area of a cocktail nestled in a Nick and Nora also helps keep it colder for longer.

WINE AND SPRITZ GLASSES

For spritzes—cocktails made with sparkling wine—you have a few options. Big red wine glasses are fun and totally functional if that's what you already have at home—as long as they are large enough to fit both the cocktail and the ice. For spritzes without ice, you can use a coupe or a Champagne glass. For drinks like the Red Lips and Rosy Cheeks (page 91), a spritz-style goblet is best: You can load it up with ice to keep things nice and cold while you sip leisurely.

OLD-FASHIONED GLASSES

For drinks that are shaken or stirred and served on ice, an old-fashioned glass or a double old-fashioned glass is the way to go. These come in various designs and colors, so aesthetic decisions are up to you. Size matters, though. If you will be serving cocktails on 1-inch ice cubes or cubes from your ice machine at home, you can typically use a smaller (6- to 8-ounce) old-fashioned glass and have plenty of room for the ice and the cocktail, plus a citrus peel garnish. If you enjoy a single large cube or sphere, which are in vogue in cocktail bars these days, use a double old-fashioned glass, which is large enough to accommodate both the cocktail and the large rock.

COLLINS AND HIGHBALL GLASSES

For drinks that include soda or sparkling water, use a Collins or highball glass. While these glasses look alike—they're both tall—a highball glass is better suited for two-ingredient drinks, like a Diet Coke and vodka or a whiskey and ginger beer, because the shape is shorter and narrower. A (taller, wider) Collins glass is better suited for more complicated cocktails that also include citrus juice or liqueurs because they can hold more liquid and/or more ice. Size-wise, aim for something that holds at least 10 to 12 ounces—most fizzy Collins-style drinks will be in the 7- to 8-ounce range, so you want to have enough room to include ice.

SHOT GLASSES

There are a few playful shots in this book, so be armed and ready for the occasion with a set of your most fabulous shot glasses. Pro tip: The internet is full of options that are etched with Tay lyrics, so do a little googling to find one that best matches your style!

SPIRITS & LIQUEURS

In the recipes in this book, you'll see brand names indicated when that product's specific formula brings something unique to the mix. Consider these as top recommendations but not always hard-and-fast rules. Here are some insights into why some ingredients get called out by name, and what you can do if you don't want to buy that specific bottle. (These ingredients are all used more than once in this book.)

ABSINTHE

One of the booze world's most dramatic spirits, absinthe is made with a medley of herbs, including wormwood, anise, and fennel. It is usually high-proof and it packs a massive punch of flavor, so it's used sparingly in drinks.

* SINKING SHIPS (PAGE 92)
* ROSE FROM THE DEAD (PAGE 105)
* STOLEN LULLABY (PAGE 129)

AMARO

Italian distillers have been making the bitter liqueurs called amaro for centuries. Made with an array of spices, herbs, and other botanicals, their key characteristic is bitterness, though they can also taste quite sweet thanks to added sugar. The drinks in this book that call for amaro benefit most from one that has a nice, even balance, like those made by Nonino, Averna, Luxardo, or Ramazzotti. When a recipe specifies a brand, like Fernet-Branca for example, that's because the product brings a specific quality to the mix that best complements the other ingredients in the drink, so while you *could* use a different amaro, the cocktail will taste like its most authentic self with the recommended brand.

* TEAM JACOB (PAGE 57)
* IN SCREAMING COLOR (PAGE 84)
* LET THE GAMES BEGIN (PAGE 98)
* THE BEST OF ME (PAGE 169)

ANGOSTURA BITTERS

The most iconic brand of bitters on the market, dating back to the 1800s, Angostura tastes like a big wallop of baking spices—clove, nutmeg, allspice—and so it's used in the minuscule measurements called dashes. Angostura bridges the gap between booze and citrus or other ingredients seamlessly: It's like adding salt to a dish to bring together the flavors and make them pop. Angostura bitters come in small or large bottles sold at liquor stores (and sometimes in grocery stores, depending on state law). There are many new-school brands that have launched their own versions of aromatic bitters, and while some of them would work in the cocktails in this book in a pinch, there's no true substitute for the original.

* WISHING STAR (PAGE 34)
* SELF-PRESERVATION (PAGE 47)
* FIREWORKS SHOW (PAGE 54)
* FOR YOU (PAGE 62)
* BUUUURN! (PAGE 88)
* LET THE GAMES BEGIN (PAGE 98)
* ROSE FROM THE DEAD (PAGE 105)
* FEVER DREAM (PAGE 110)
* FOREVER AND EVER (PAGE 113)
* STOLEN LULLABY (PAGE 129)
* ONLY SEVENTEEN (PAGE 133)
* T-SWIZZLE'S TEA SWIZZLE (PAGE 146)

ANGOSTURA COCOA BITTERS

The cocoa notes of Angostura cocoa bitters—one of the newest flavors in the Angostura family—ring close to baking chocolate: a bit dry and dusty yet with a nice, rich roundness. Other chocolate bitters on the market could substitute for these. (If you don't want two types of cocoa bitters in the house, you might choose between these and the chipotle-cacao bitters from Bittercube. The latter have a kick of heat, so if you don't like spicy takes on the following cocktails, use the Angostura version!)

* WISHING STAR (PAGE 34)
* STOLEN LULLABY (PAGE 129)
* MIRACLE MOVE-ON DRUG (PAGE 158)

BÉNÉDICTINE

Made in France from a recipe that dates to the nineteenth century, Bénédictine is an extremely complex liqueur featuring honeyed notes of baking spice, orange peel, and other botanicals, including flowers, herbs, and roots. It tastes quite mild compared to other herbal liqueurs like Chartreuse, and it's almost syrupy compared to many modern liqueurs. Classically used in the Vieux Carré cocktail, it brings an ethereal elegance to stirred drinks.

* FOREVER AND EVER (PAGE 113)
* MINE TO LOSE (PAGE 130)

BITTERCUBE CHIPOTLE-CACAO BITTERS

With a little sweet heat from chipotle peppers, these are a fabulous option for adding a warm kick to cocktails like old-fashioneds and margaritas. If you already have other spicy bitters at home, you can experiment with those instead. Hellfire Habanero Shrub from Bittermens is also versatile and would work great in any of these recipes; or, if you already bought Angostura cocoa bitters, you could use those (though you'll lose that spicy factor). Because bitters are used in such small quantities, these choices won't make a major difference in the cocktails. It's your call.

* TAKE US TO CHURCH (PAGE 101)
* PETER LOSING WENDY (PAGE 122)
* SPELL CASTER (PAGE 134)

CAMPARI AND APEROL

These red Italian liqueurs have the most beautiful color, and they bring a light citrusy tartness to cocktails like the Aperol spritz and the Negroni. With different botanical profiles and amounts of sugar, they are not typically interchangeable, so if a recipe calls for one or the other it's wisest to follow that recommendation. Specifically, Campari has a punchier bitterness, while Aperol has more sweetness and a softer, lighter presence in the glass.

* CARELESS MAN'S CAREFUL DAUGHTER (PAGE 53)
* FRESH START (PAGE 76)
* IN SCREAMING COLOR (PAGE 84)
* BUUUURN! (PAGE 88)
* RED LIPS AND ROSY CHEEKS (PAGE 91)
* TACTICAL TONIC (PAGE 154)

CHINOLA PASSION FRUIT LIQUEUR

Named after the Dominican Spanish word for "passion fruit," this liqueur is made with 100 percent fresh fruit and cane spirit with no artificial colors or flavors—which makes every drink it touches taste like the real deal. Many other passion fruit liqueurs on the market are made with artificial flavorings, and the difference between those bottom-shelf options and Chinola is like night and day. Don't use the cheap stuff!

* FOR YOU (PAGE 62)
* CHILDLESS CAT LADY (PAGE 118)
* T-SWIZZLE'S TEA SWIZZLE (PAGE 146)

COCCHI AMERICANO AND LILLET BLANC

These white wine–based aperitifs are beautiful liqueurs that taste wonderful on their own or served with soda and ice, and they bring a kiss of floral sweetness to cocktails. Both have bright citrus notes and bouquets of subtle herbaceous complexity. Cocchi Americano, an Italian liqueur that's been produced since 1891, has a slight edge from cinchona bark (used to make tonic water), a rich sweetness, and a soft vanilla note. Lillet Blanc, made with a base of Sémillon and Sauvignon Blanc grapes (in addition to others), leans comparatively dry, with orange blossom notes. Each has a slightly different personality, but you can use them interchangeably if your budget does not allow for both. Just remember to keep the bottles in the fridge when you're not using them, so they stay cold and fresh.

* FOREVERMORE (PAGE 106)
* CRESTFALLEN CURE (PAGE 137)
* FRENCH BLONDIE (PAGE 165)

COFFEE LIQUEUR

Kahlua is the OG coffee liqueur. Made in Mexico with a base of rum and arabica coffee, it is a solid workhorse for many classic cocktails (espresso martini, white Russian, et cetera). The recipes in this book were developed with Kahlua, so they will all taste good with that liqueur. These days, distillers across the US are experimenting with making new-school coffee liqueurs. Many of these use high-quality coffee, so if you're a coffee drinker who appreciates brews with more complexity than Kahlua offers, it might be worth trying something new. Just know that many modern coffee liqueurs have less sugar than Kahlua; you might need to add a little simple syrup to a recipe to keep the balance in check. This is a taste-as-you-go situation.

* F*CK THE PATRIARCHY (PAGE 71)
* FRESH START (PAGE 76)
* NOT-SO-STYLISH ENDING (PAGE 95)
* THE BEST OF ME (PAGE 169)

CRÈME DE CACAO

Crème de cacao is a historic chocolate-flavored liqueur made with cacao. Tempus Fugit's version of the liqueur is made with cacao from Venezuela and vanilla from Mexico, based on a nineteenth-century recipe featuring ingredients from those origins; no artificial colors or flavorings are added. With a rich, syrupy texture, it's a decadent, complex liqueur that brings an impressive boost of sweet dark chocolate to modern cocktails. You could also use Giffard's white version of crème de cacao, which has a more delicate texture and a flavor that tastes like soft, floral milk chocolate without the heavy vanilla spice notes of Tempus Fugit. Both are great options for the drinks in this book.

* MASERATI NEGRONI (PAGE 67)
* MIRACLE MOVE-ON DRUG (PAGE 158)

ELDERFLOWER LIQUEUR

Elderflower liqueur captures the singsongy floral notes of the fresh white flowers of the elderberry bush. Today other elderflower liqueurs are available, but the iconic St-Germain remains the industry standard, thanks to its pitch-perfect balance. The French liqueur is made with fresh-picked flowers once a year. Giffard makes a wild elderflower liqueur that is also delicious, as well as an alcohol-free version of the liqueur that can be used in these drinks to make them zero-proof.

* PLAY IT AGAIN (PAGE 38)
* ONLY SEVENTEEN (PAGE 133)
* FRENCH BLONDIE (PAGE 165)

DOLIN BLANC VERMOUTH

Vermouths come in various styles—extra dry, dry, blanc, and sweet. While dry and sweet are the most common, blanc vermouth sits between the two with a soft balance of flavor that works well in cocktails. Dolin is one of the only brands that brings a blanc version to the US market; made with more than two dozen botanicals including cinnamon, basil, and gentian from the Alps, it has a silky-smooth mouthfeel. As is the case with other fortified wines, store vermouth in the fridge to preserve its freshness.

* JAMES DEAN DAYDREAM (PAGE 83)
* SINKING SHIPS (PAGE 92)
* 1-2-3, LET'S GO B*TCH (PAGE 102)
* SAPPHIRE MARTINI (PAGE 150)

GREEN CHARTREUSE

A classic component of iconic cocktails like the Last Word, the Bijou, and the Champs-Élysées, green Chartreuse is made by Carthusian monks in France using a recipe that dates to 1764. It is a high-proof liqueur that buzzes with strong botanicals and a hearty alpine sweetness. There is no perfect substitute for the original, but as it can be harder to find these days than it used to be, there are a few near-substitutes you can try, including BROVO Uncharted Rhapsody American Forest Liqueur or Faccia Brutto Centerbe.

* SINKING SHIPS (PAGE 92)
* PAPER CUT STINGS (PAGE 114)
* SPELL CASTER (PAGE 134)

LUXARDO MARASCHINO LIQUEUR

Cherry liqueurs come in all colors and sweetness levels, but the most interesting (and luxurious) one comes from the Luxardo company in Padua, Italy. Their maraschino liqueur is made with marasca cherries and leaves and branches from the same trees, creating a wildly complex snapshot of "cherry" that's nothing like the artificial, too-sweet versions that often line the bottom shelves of liquor stores. Because this liqueur has a multidimensional flavor profile (some nutty qualities and others ranging from white flowers to orange marmalade), using another cherry liqueur will change the flavor of the cocktail dramatically. Use this if you possibly can when it's called for in a recipe.

* MOJITO 22 (PAGE 72)
* JAMES DEAN DAYDREAM (PAGE 83)
* MIRACLE MOVE-ON DRUG (PAGE 158)
* FLO! FLORIDA! FLORIDITA! (PAGE 162)

LUXARDO MARASCHINO CHERRIES

Luxardo also makes cocktail cherries, which come in a jar of the most decadent cherry syrup you'll ever taste. They are more expensive than the neon-red maraschino cherries you'll find in grocery stores, but the splurge is worth it! Not only do the cherries bring a top-shelf quality to cocktails as a garnish, they are irresistible to eat on their own or over ice cream. You can also add a bit of the cherry syrup to drinks like the classic Manhattan or the Mojito 22 on page 72. Trust.

* JAMES DEAN DAYDREAM (PAGE 83)
* INSULT TO INJURY (PAGE 126)
* SPELL CASTER (PAGE 134)
* MIRACLE MOVE-ON DRUG (PAGE 158)

PEYCHAUD'S BITTERS

One of the most frequently used types of bitters in the cocktail world (next to orange bitters and Angostura), bright-pink Peychaud's brings a slightly medicinal fennel, mint, and vanilla flavor to cocktails. In a pinch, you could use orange bitters in these drinks instead.

* WONDERSTRUCK (PAGE 61)
* SNAKES AND STONES (PAGE 117)
* VIOLET LOVE SPIRAL (PAGE 142)

ORANGE LIQUEUR

Orange liqueurs range from thin and sticky (because they are made with artificial flavorings and a base of neutral grain spirits like Everclear) to rich, complex, and robust (when made with a base spirit like brandy or Cognac, plus real orange peels and high-quality spices). The cocktails in this book taste best with Ferrand dry curaçao, a classy upgrade that takes drinks from basic to bar-quality in a jiffy. Based on a recipe from the nineteenth century, it has a Cognac-and-brandy base that's blended with spices and the peels of bitter oranges from Curaçao. It tastes beautifully rich and complex. (You could also use this in the Benjamin Button shot on page 118 instead of blue curaçao—it will make the most elegant version of that drink, though without the bright blue color.) If you want to use a different orange liqueur, Grand Marnier and Cointreau Black are also made with a brandy base, so those would be the most seamless swap (though they both taste somewhat sweeter than Ferrand).

* FIREWORKS SHOW (PAGE 54)
* CHILDLESS CAT LADY (PAGE 118)
* HOLIDAY HOUSE (PAGE 125)

SYRUPS

Most cocktails call for a syrup to bring balance to ingredients like booze and citrus juice. Commercial options are available for almost all of these, so you can buy them online or at a grocery store if you don't want to make them at home—just look at the ingredients list before buying, and avoid the ones with long lists of artificial ingredients. The purest syrups will have sugar, water, flavorings (natural ones are best), and maybe a basic preservative, and that's it.

Always store syrups in the refrigerator, where they should stay usable for about two weeks.

SIMPLE SYRUP

The standard sweetener for cocktails of all kinds, simple syrup (just water and sugar) can be made with raw cane sugar or white refined sugar. The former will have a bit more flavor and personality than the latter, which will taste almost neutral. Many recipes call for heating the ingredients in a pan on a stove, but when you simply shake the ingredients together until combined, it has a thicker texture and more vibrant sweetness.

1 CUP SUGAR
1 CUP WATER

Make it:

Combine the sugar and water in a mason jar or other container with a lid. Close the lid tightly and shake the mixture until all particles of sugar have disappeared. When you pick it up to mix cocktails, give it a few brief shakes to integrate any granules that might have settled at the bottom of the jar. *(Makes 1½ cups)*

Use it:
* WISHING STAR (PAGE 34)
* TAKE ME BACK (PAGE 37)
* PLAY IT AGAIN (PAGE 38)
* MARRY ME, JULIET (PAGE 44)
* WONDERSTRUCK (PAGE 61)
* MOJITO 22 (PAGE 72)
* NEVER SAY NEVER (PAGE 75)
* JAMES DEAN DAYDREAM (PAGE 83)
* TAKE US TO CHURCH (PAGE 101)
* PAPER CUT STINGS (PAGE 114)
* CRESTFALLEN CURE (PAGE 137)
* SCARLET RUST (PAGE 145)
* YOYOKOLADA (PAGE 149)
* FLO! FLORIDA! FLORIDITA! (PAGE 162)
* FRENCH BLONDIE (PAGE 165)

DEMERARA SYRUP

Cocktails made with aged spirits like whiskey, brandy, and rum need a more substantial sweetener than those made with highly refined sugars. Demerara syrup is made with sugar that has been minimally processed, so it retains more color and flavor than other sugars. In appearance it's slightly lighter than brown sugar.

1 CUP DEMERARA SUGAR
1 CUP WATER

Make it:

Combine the sugar and water in a mason jar or other container with a lid. Shake the mixture until all particles of sugar have disappeared. When you pick it up to mix cocktails, give it a few brief shakes to integrate any granules that might have settled at the bottom of the jar. *(Makes 1½ cups)*

Use it:
* OLD HICKORY LAKE (PAGE 33)
* SELF-PRESERVATION (PAGE 47)
* FEVER DREAM (PAGE 110)
* ONLY SEVENTEEN (PAGE 133)
* STORMY SOLILOQUY (PAGE 161)

HONEY SYRUP

Honey syrup boosts cocktails with a rich sweetness and lovely floral quality. In its normal state, honey's texture is too thick to integrate into a drink easily: Making a honey syrup thins the viscosity so it better blends with other liquids. The typical ratio is four parts honey to one part water. The following recipe gives quantities for one 12-ounce honey bear's worth of honey; it will make more than a dozen cocktails. You can taste and adjust your ratios as you like.

```
12 OUNCES HONEY
3 OUNCES WARM WATER
```

Make it:

In a mason jar or other container that can be sealed, combine the honey and water (make sure it is warmer than room temperature for best results). Stir the mixture briefly to integrate the water into the honey, then close the lid and shake until the honey is incorporated with no clumps remaining, and the viscosity looks smooth. *(Makes 1 cup)*

Use it:

* FEARLESS 13 (PAGE 43)
* IN SCREAMING COLOR (PAGE 84)
* MY KIND OF REBELLION (PAGE 87)
* LET THE GAMES BEGIN (PAGE 88)
* THE GUY ON THE CHIEFS (PAGE 153)

BLACK TEA SYRUP

The rich tannins in black tea bring a vigorous backbone to cocktails made with aged spirits like rum, whiskey, and brandy. They also work swimmingly in hot cocktails like a toddy or hot chocolate. If you want the most straightforward black tea character in the cocktail, use English, Irish, or Scottish breakfast tea. If you want to get more creative or put your personal spin on it, you could use the bergamot-spiked Earl Grey, or another black tea featuring additional flavorings.

```
1 CUP BOILING WATER
1 TEA BAG BLACK TEA
1 CUP SUGAR
```

Make it:

Combine the water and teabag in a mason jar or other glass container with a lid. Steep for about 4 minutes so the flavor is strong. Remove the teabag and add the sugar, then shake to dissolve the granules. *(Makes 1½ cups)*

Use it:

* MINE TO LOSE (PAGE 130)
* T-SWIZZLE'S TEA SWIZZLE (PAGE 146)

CINNAMON SYRUP

Warm cinnamon spice works well with aged spirits like whiskey, rum, brandy, and tequila. It's a natural pairing for comforting cold-weather cocktails, but it also brings a surprisingly zippy note to tropical cocktails and to citrusy shaken cocktails that have complementary flavors like grapefruit and lemon. The trick is to decide how much cinnamon flavor you want in the syrup. If you really like cinnamon, let it steep for a longer time (about 20 minutes) so the character comes out swinging. If you steep it relatively lightly instead (more like 15 minutes), this syrup is subtle and curious, working almost as a neutral texture booster.

3 (3- TO 4-INCH) CINNAMON STICKS
1 CUP SUGAR
1 CUP WATER

Make it:

Because cinnamon bark is tough and doesn't infuse into syrup easily, this recipe will be made on the stovetop in a saucepan. First, break up the cinnamon sticks into smaller pieces. Place them in a small saucepan over medium-high heat and toast the cinnamon bark until it starts to smell toasted, about 3 minutes. Keep an eye on this process, stirring the bark occasionally so pieces don't burn but toast evenly. Once the spice starts to smell aromatic and toasted, turn off the heat and let the pan cool slightly, about 5 minutes (if you add the water immediately, it might sputter and splash). Once the pan is cool-ish, add the water and sugar to the bark and turn the heat back up to high. Stir as the liquid comes to a boil, to make sure the sugar doesn't burn as the pan warms. Keep stirring at a boil until the sugar dissolves, then turn off the heat and remove the pan from the burner. Let the cinnamon bark steep in the syrup for 15 to 20 minutes. Strain the bark out and let the syrup cool completely before using. *(Makes 1½ cups)*

Use it:

* CARELESS MAN'S CAREFUL DAUGHTER (PAGE 53)
* ROSE FROM THE DEAD (PAGE 105)
* PETER LOSING WENDY (PAGE 122)
* AMBER SKIES (PAGE 138)

LAVENDER SYRUP

Soft fresh lavender makes this syrup sing soprano. It's a great option for sweetening a simple lemonade or for bringing a subtle floral note to the cocktails in this book. If possible, use fresh lavender for best results, but if you don't have access to fresh plants, buy culinary-grade dried lavender flowers online.

1 CUP WATER
1 CUP SUGAR
2 SPRIGS FRESH LAVENDER OR
  1 TABLESPOON DRIED LAVENDER
  FLOWERS

Make it:

Bring the water to a boil in a saucepan, then add the sugar and lavender. Reduce the heat to medium-high and stir until the sugar dissolves. Remove from the heat. Let sit for 5 minutes. Remove the lavender sprigs and strain the syrup into a container with a lid. Let cool before using. *(Makes 1½ cups)*

Use it:

* STOLEN LULLABY (PAGE 129)
* VIOLET LOVE SPIRAL (PAGE 142)

GRENADINE

Grenadine is a beautiful pomegranate juice–based syrup that brings a lush richness to cocktails. It can be made in many different ways. Most include a bit of orange flower water for a layer of light floral complexity, but to keep things simple you can omit that ingredient if you prefer (it can be overpowering if you add too much). In step with the way some cocktail bars make their grenadine, this recipe is half-fresh and half-cooked, because 100 percent fresh grenadine can be too perky, while 100 percent cooked grenadine can sometimes taste too dark and thick. This fifty-fifty mix strikes just the right balance for the cocktails in this book.

2 CUPS POMEGRANATE JUICE
1½ CUPS SUGAR

Make it:

Add 1 cup of the pomegranate juice to a pan. Bring to a boil, then reduce the heat to medium and let simmer gently for 12 to 15 minutes, until it has reduced by half. Remove from the heat and add the remaining 1 cup pomegranate juice and the sugar. Stir until the sugar is dissolved. Remove from the heat and let cool before using. *(Makes 2¼ cups)*

Use it:

* COLD HARD GROUND (PAGE 68)
* LIGHTS ARE SO BRIGHT (PAGE 80)
* ROSE FROM THE DEAD (PAGE 105)
* CHILDLESS CAT LADY (PAGE 118)

T-SWIFT TRIVIA

A person could write an entire encyclopedia of fun facts about Blondie these days, but here are a few of our faves.

★ Taylor's mom, Andrea, named her after the famous singer-songwriter James Taylor. She wanted to give her daughter a gender-neutral name because she wanted Taylor to be taken seriously in the business world, and she believed she'd get a better shot at that if people didn't immediately know she was a woman.

★ In 2019, she played Bombalurina in the film version of the musical Cats.

★ The first song Taylor learned how to play on the guitar was "Kiss Me" by Sixpence None the Richer.

★ As a billionaire, she regularly donates money to charities, including environmental disaster relief funds, sexual assault survivor support organizations, pet rescue organizations, and food banks.

★ Universities including Stanford, Colorado State, Berkeley, UT Austin, and Rice have all featured courses based on Swift's storytelling and songwriting.

★ The Eras Tour video debuted in 8,500 AMC Theatres in more than 100 countries around the world. When it hit the streaming network Disney+, it became the No. 1 music film ever appearing on the platform, with 4.6 million views.

★ She wrote "This Is What You Came For" with Calvin Harris under the pseudonym Nils Sjöberg, so people would only focus on the song and not on her relationship with Harris.

★ The Eras Tour covered 146 dates over five continents, drawing an average of 72,000 fans per night and grossing more than $2 billion.

★ Friends is her favorite TV show of all time; Love Actually is her favorite movie.

★ The nickname her younger brother, Austin, gave her is Teffy.

Taylor Swift

(2006)

With the debut of Taylor Swift's self-titled album in 2006, we fell in love with the starry-eyed sixteen-year-old from Pennsylvania as she navigated the highs and lows of teenage life with her guitar and notebook. Through whirlwind summer romances and wistful stories of unrequited love, hits like "Tim McGraw" and "Teardrops on My Guitar" hinted that a star was born. As a toast to this era, the cocktails in this group are simple, refreshing drinks, many of them colored with a laid-back Southern drawl. From the whiskey sour–inspired Old Hickory Lake (page 33) to the tall glass of vodka-spiked iced tea (Take Me Back, page 37), when tied together with a smile they're best sipped with feet kicked up on a summer patio, soft breeze rustling through your hair.

★ *Taylor lived in Nashville during this time, and her style was defined by cowboy boots, big fabulous curls, and a guitar always in her hands.*

★ *In 2007, she won the Horizon Award at the Country Music Awards ceremony, where she performed "Online" with Brad Paisley and Kellie Pickler.*

★ *She cut her chops opening for legendary country artists, including Tim McGraw, Kenny Chesney, George Strait, and Faith Hill.*

Old Hickory Lake

This sweet glass of refreshment is the perfect antidote to the blues that creep in as summer love fades into the rearview mirror. Think of it like a whiskey sour with a thick Southern accent—the peaches pair perfectly with the vanilla and oak notes of the whiskey, and lemon juice keeps the mix bright and perky. When you take a sip, imagine lying in the bed of an old Chevy truck with your high school crush, looking up at the stars, listening to your favorite song.

2 OUNCES BOURBON

3/4 OUNCE FRESH LEMON JUICE

3/4 OUNCE DEMERARA SYRUP (PAGE 25)

1 PEACH, PEELED, PITTED, AND CUT INTO QUARTERS

BIG BOUQUET OF MINT

Place the bouquet of mint and the peach quarters in a shaker tin and muddle them to smash up the fruit and mix the mint into the pulp. Add the demerara syrup, lemon juice, and bourbon and shake to combine. Double-strain into an old-fashioned glass filled with crushed ice: Hold a fine-mesh strainer underneath the Hawthorne strainer as you strain, to make sure no bits of fruit end up in the drink. Serve and think happiness.

YOUR (N/A) VERSION: *To make an alcohol-free version that'll put the Georgia stars to shame, swap in Spiritless Kentucky 74, or your favorite zero-proof whiskey alternative, for the bourbon.*

Wishing Star

You don't need to fake a smile for this chocolate-covered strawberry-inspired cocktail. For times when unrequited love's got you reaching for the tissue box, it's the next best thing to wishing on a wishing star. The combination of cocoa bitters and fresh strawberries is reliably delicious, and the subdued floral notes of Hendrick's gin, which is made with roses, complement the fresh strawberry flavor nicely. One could call it kind of flawless.

2 OUNCES	GIN (PREFERABLY HENDRICK'S)
3/4 OUNCE	FRESH LEMON JUICE
3/4 OUNCE	SIMPLE SYRUP (PAGE 25)
2 DASHES	ANGOSTURA COCOA BITTERS, PLUS MORE FOR GARNISH
5	STRAWBERRIES

Halve 4 of the strawberries and add with the Angostura cocoa bitters to a shaker tin. Muddle until the strawberries resemble a chunky jam, then add the simple syrup, lemon juice, and gin. Add ice and shake to chill. Double-strain into a coupe glass: Hold a fine-mesh strainer underneath the Hawthorne strainer as you strain. Garnish with the remaining strawberry: Cut a notch in the bottom so it sits on the rim of the glass. Dash a bit of cocoa bitters on top, so the drinking experience begins with the delightful smell of chocolate. Serve to whomever you please; they will never know.

TAYLOR SPEAKS

"[Something that was] said to me early on was, 'Teenagers don't listen to country music. That's not the audience. The audience is a thirty-five-year-old housewife. . . . How are you going to relate to those women when you're sixteen years old? You should come back when you're in your twenties.' And I kept thinking, 'But I love country music, and I'm a teenager! There have to be more kids out there like me.'" —NPR, 2014

YOUR (N/A) VERSION: *You have a lot of options for zero-proof gin to use in this recipe to make it as good as the song in the car you keep singing. The "gin" from Cut Above has a bright quality that pairs well with the strawberries. All The Bitter aromatic bitters bump up the complexity, though they don't have a chocolate note like Angostura does, so the drink will lose that chocolate-covered-strawberry vibe. It's still delicious, either way.*

Take Me Back

Like a heartwarming movie montage, "Mary's Song" paints the most wonderful picture of the love of a lifetime. When it comes to whiling away hours on the front porch remembering the best times in life—falling in love with the kid next door, first kisses, first fights, marriage proposals, and rocking babies to sleep—there's no better option than a Southern sweet tea.

2 OUNCES	VODKA
3/4 OUNCE	FRESH LEMON JUICE
3/4 OUNCE	SIMPLE SYRUP (PAGE 25)
4 OUNCES	COLD, UNSWEETENED BREWED BLACK TEA
	LEMON PEEL, FOR GARNISH

Prepare a 12-ounce mason jar by filling it three-quarters of the way full with ice. Add the iced tea. Set aside. In a shaker tin, combine the simple syrup, lemon juice, and vodka. Add ice and shake to chill, then strain the cocktail into the prepared mason jar. Give it a quick stir to integrate the cocktail with the tea. Garnish by squeezing the lemon peel over the top of the drink to express the oils, then place the peel in the glass. Serve and say cheers to the 87 to your 89.

YOUR (N/A) VERSION: *Use your favorite zero-proof vodka if you want to make a facsimile of the original recipe that tastes as good as saying "I do." If you dig the lemony qualities of the drink (think: more Arnold Palmer, less sweet tea), Seedlip Grove 42 has a sunny citrus flavor that lifts up the dark notes of the tea. Use the same measure as called for in the recipe, and oh, my, my, my, you're good to go.*

Play It Again

Grab a pen and an old napkin to write down the recipe for this sparkling elderflower lemonade, because it's one you'll want in constant rotation while you live in love. Made for an easy, breezy romance—the kind that's got you riding shotgun with hair undone and the radio on, with nowhere to be and your main squeeze by your side. It tastes so good, they'll be asking if you can serve it again, amen.

2 OUNCES	GIN
3/4 OUNCE	ELDERFLOWER LIQUEUR
3/4 OUNCE	FRESH LEMON JUICE
1/2 OUNCE	SIMPLE SYRUP (PAGE 25)
1 DASH	ORANGE BITTERS (PREFERABLY SCRAPPY'S)
3 TO 5 OUNCES	CLUB SODA
	EDIBLE FLOWERS, FOR GARNISH

Fill a Collins glass about three-quarters full with ice, then add 3 ounces of club soda. Set aside. In a shaker tin, combine the orange bitters, simple syrup, lemon juice, elderflower liqueur, and gin with ice. Shake to chill, then strain into the prepared Collins glass. Take a sip—if it's too sweet for you, add 1 or 2 more ounces of club soda. Garnish with edible flowers and sip *reeeaal* slow, 'cause it's late and your momma don't know.

YOUR (N/A) VERSION: *If you are making the alcohol-free version of this drink, use a nonalcoholic gin option (Monday Zero is recommended) in place of the spirit, plus the zero-proof elderflower liqueur from Giffard. All The Bitter orange bitters is a seamless swap—use one dropperful of bitters for the same effect.*

TAYLOR SPEAKS
"Fearless was an album full of magic and curiosity, the bliss and devastation of youth. . . . It was the diary of the adventures and explorations of a teenage girl who was learning tiny lessons with every new crack in the facade of the fairy-tale ending she'd been shown in the movies."
—TASTE OF COUNTRY, 2021

FEARLESS

(2008)

If her self-titled album lit the spark of fame, *Fearless* fanned the flames, making Taylor a bona fide household name with smash hits like "You Belong With Me," "White Horse," "Fearless," and "Love Story." As her songwriting started to veer slightly beyond the typical Nashville sound, this era also marked her first headlining tour (complete with that red-lip classic look that she'd keep as a signature style) and her first forays into the world of major awards and accolades. As a tribute to the way Taylor stayed down-to-earth as she continued to come into her own in this era, the cocktails in this chapter include lighthearted, easygoing sippers (such as Marry Me, Juliet on page 44) and a playful beer-and-a-shot combo (You Beer-long with Me, page 48).

★ *She won several of her first Grammys, including her first Album of the Year. At twenty years old, she was, at the time, the youngest artist to ever win the award.*

★ *As she became a rising star in both country and pop music, mainstream media started to pay closer attention to her personal life, including her high-profile relationships with John Mayer and Taylor Lautner.*

★ *During this era, she shifted her style from simple white dresses and cowboy boots to sparkling fringe dresses, big princess ballgowns, and rhinestone-clad guitars. She also sketched her lucky number, 13, on the back of her hand for each performance on the* Fearless *tour.*

FEARLESS 13

Hands up in a heart shape for this shimmering homage to Tay's *Fearless* era, because it doesn't get much better than this. In a twist on the classic French 75, sparkling wine flutters in like the butterflies that come along with first love; Cognac takes the stage instead of gin, because its warm toffee and leather notes cuddle up well to the lemon juice; and in honor of how Taylor adopted a wardrobe of bright glittering gold-fringe dresses during this era, the cocktail features honey syrup instead of simple syrup. In this moment now: Capture it, remember it!

2 OUNCES	COGNAC (PREFERABLY FERRAND 1840)
3/4 OUNCE	FRESH LEMON JUICE
1 OUNCE	HONEY SYRUP (PAGE 26)
	GOLD EDIBLE GLITTER (OPTIONAL)
4 OUNCES	CHAMPAGNE OR SPARKLING WINE
	LEMON TWIST, FOR GARNISH

Pour the Champagne or sparkling wine into a coupe or Champagne flute; set aside. In a shaker tin, combine the edible glitter (if using), honey syrup, lemon juice, and Cognac. Shake with ice to chill, then strain into the prepared glass. To garnish, place the lemon twist on the edge of the flute. Serve in your best dress, fearless.

YOUR (N/A) VERSION: *Alcohol-free brandy options can be harder to find than other base-spirit categories, so if you can find one to use here, you'll be ready to dance in that storm. If not, zero-proof whiskeys bring the same warm vanilla and oak notes to the glass. Try Spiritless Kentucky 74 or Cut Above Spirits zero-proof whiskey—both have a great backbone of oak and vanilla. For the wine, options abound, but the cocktail tastes especially complex and balanced with Thomson & Scott's Noughty Alcohol-Free Sparkling Chardonnay or Pierre Zéro sparkling Chardonnay from Maison Chavin.*

MARRY ME, JULIET

The clever way Taylor reenvisions Shakespeare's *Romeo and Juliet* in "Love Story" demands a drink that tastes just as swoon-worthy. This refreshing shaken number that spotlights fresh basil and Hendrick's—a gin made with roses and cucumbers—channels the vibes of sneaking out to the garden to meet your Romeo in the middle of the night. For princes and princesses alike, all you've got to do is just say yes. Don't have a Romeo in your life yet? Don't worry . . . someday you'll find this.

2 OUNCES	GIN (PREFERABLY HENDRICK'S)
3/4 OUNCE	FRESH LIME JUICE
3/4 OUNCE	SIMPLE SYRUP (PAGE 25)
2	SLICES CUCUMBER
	BOUQUET OF BASIL
	CUCUMBER WHEEL, FOR GARNISH

Muddle the basil and cucumber slices together in a shaker tin, then add the simple syrup, lime juice, and gin, plus ice. Shake to chill, then double-strain into a coupe glass: Hold a fine-mesh strainer underneath the Hawthorne strainer as you strain. Garnish with a cucumber wheel, cut with a notch so it sits on the rim of the glass. Serve and toast to a happily ever after.

YOUR (N/A) VERSION: *To go the zero-proof route with this refreshing drink, try any of your favorite alcohol-free gin substitutes in place of the Hendrick's. For example, Monday Zero's alcohol-free gin has a sturdy, robust presence in the glass, while Cut Above's softer personality syncs up nicely with the cucumbers—the latter tastes particularly good on a balcony in summer air.*

TAYLOR SPEAKS
"I'm intimidated by the fear of being average."
—THE *TODAY* SHOW, 2006

SELF-PRESERVATION

Not every love story has a fairy-tale ending, and in cases where it's too late for the prince to ride in on a white horse and sweep you off your feet, maybe the next best option is the liquid version of happily ever after. In this warm apple pie–inspired old-fashioned, a medley of vanilla, oak, pear, and orange notes come together in perfect harmony to take the edge off the heartbreak that comes with the realization that this isn't Hollywood, it's just a small town.

2 OUNCES	APPLE BRANDY
3/4 OUNCE	ST. GEORGE SPICED PEAR LIQUEUR
1	BARSPOON DEMERARA SYRUP (PAGE 25).
2 DASHES	ORANGE BITTERS (PREFERABLY SCRAPPY'S)
	LEMON PEEL

In a mixing glass, combine the orange bitters, demerara syrup, spiced pear liqueur, and apple brandy with ice and stir to chill. Strain into an old-fashioned glass over fresh ice cubes. Squeeze the lemon peel over the top of the drink to express its oils and discard the peel. Serve, leaving that small town in the rearview.

FROM THE VAULT: *St. George spiced pear liqueur comes in two sizes, so you can buy the smaller one if you're only making a few of these. If you can't find the product, you can use Licor 43 in its place—it's on the sweeter side, so reduce the measurement to ½ ounce and skip the demerara syrup.*

YOU BEER-LONG WITH ME

"You Belong With Me" turned into an early-2000s anthem for teenagers everywhere who didn't want to conform to popular standards of femininity, during a time when Hollywood pushed a singular vision of how a woman should (and shouldn't) act. Taylor herself enjoys the occasional beer—remember when she was seen chugging one out of a plastic cup at the 2024 Super Bowl?—so this is an easygoing combo that's good for when high heels and short skirts just don't feel right. Beer and whiskey go together like your favorite T-shirt and sneakers—a timeless combination that proves that what you're looking for has been here the whole time. Best served alongside a piece of chicken with ketchup and seemingly ranch.

1 LIGHT BEER (PREFERABLY MILLER LITE)

1-1/2 OUNCES WHISKEY

Pour the whiskey into a shot glass. Pour the light beer into a plastic cup and serve both; chugging optional.

YOUR (N/A) VERSION *This recipe features Miller Lite because we think that was Taylor's beer of choice at the big game—plus whiskey because we know she loves a good dram—but you can turn this boozy combo into an alcohol-free boilermaker with ease, if you please. Non-alcoholic beers run the gamut these days, but the many different styles from Athletic Brewing pair swimmingly with the wide spectrum of N/A spirits now available. Get creative with it: Zero-proof tequila and Athletic lager practically belong together. A dark stout and shot of whiskey? Yep, those too! Hey, isn't this easy?*

TAYLOR SPEAKS

"The songs that came from this time in my life were marked by their brutal honesty, unfiltered diaristic confessions and wild wistfulness. I love this album because it tells a tale of growing up, flailing, flying and crashing . . . and living to speak about it."

—INSTAGRAM POST, MAY 2023

Speak Now

(2010)

Speak Now proved to be a pivotal moment in T-Swift's career— when the public started to see her as a permanent fixture in the music industry and not just a cute little country singer on the verge of success. As a young woman entering her twenties, she took the reins of songwriting over entirely and her lyrics started to mature. This is the first album she wrote solo, with each song representing an open letter to someone she knows, telling them something she couldn't say in person. With the album selling a million copies in the first week, propelling tracks like "Enchanted," "Mine," "Mean," "Sparks Fly," and "Back to December" into the spotlight, she proved to everyone that she wasn't going anywhere anytime soon.

In the same key, the recipes in this chapter are a little more advanced than previous ones—more punchy and confident. Each one also spotlights a particularly notable ingredient— like Campari in the Careless Man's Careful Daughter on page 53, or passion fruit liqueur in the For You on page 62—because each one has something serious to say within the context of its glass-mates.

★ *Piggybacking on the success of "Enchanted," Swift launched a line of perfume called Wonderstruck.*

★ *The track "Mean" morphed into an anti-bullying anthem on a national level, helping schoolkids everywhere overcome adversity.*

★ *The world tour for Speak Now was a headline grabber as she visited more than 75 cities in 17 countries—selling out every one—and invited guest singers like Justin Bieber, Nicki Minaj, and Hayley Williams on stage for duets.*

Careless Man's Careful Daughter

As we start to ease out of Taylor's country days and into songs that have a little more of a poppy kick, this uplifting tequila-and-grapefruit combo is so surprisingly refreshing, every sip feels like trying it for the first time. Can you believe it? The cocktail starts warm and comfy thanks to the cinnamon syrup, then it lights up with a small zap of Campari—an Italian liqueur so bold it'll make a rebel of any careless man's careful daughter. Give it a leap of faith—it could just be the best thing you've ever tried.

2 OUNCES   REPOSADO TEQUILA

1/2 OUNCE CAMPARI

3/4 OUNCE GRAPEFRUIT JUICE

1/2 OUNCE FRESH LIME JUICE

1/2 OUNCE CINNAMON SYRUP
           (PAGE 27)

1 DASH   GRAPEFRUIT BITTERS

           GRAPEFRUIT TWIST,
           FOR GARNISH

In a shaker tin, combine the grapefruit bitters, cinnamon syrup, lime and grapefruit juices, Campari, and tequila. Add ice and shake to chill, then strain into a coupe glass. Garnish by placing the grapefruit twist on the rim of the glass. Serve and hold on, make it last.

Fireworks Show

Drop everything now for this captivating cocktail, which contrasts the marmalade-orange notes of curaçao with nutty orgeat, a kick of wild whiskey, and a whisper of bitters. It's like locking eyes with your crush for the first time, or like the rush that comes with seeing a gorgeous smile: There's an electric flash that happens when you light the cinnamon garnish on fire. Let the sparks fly!

2 OUNCES	WHISKEY
3/4 OUNCE	ORANGE LIQUEUR (PREFERABLY FERRAND DRY CURAÇAO)
3/4 OUNCE	ORGEAT
3/4 OUNCE	FRESH LEMON JUICE
	ANGOSTURA BITTERS
	ORANGE WHEEL, FOR GARNISH
	CINNAMON STICK, FOR GARNISH

In a shaker tin, combine a dash of the Angostura bitters, the lemon juice, orgeat, orange liqueur, and whiskey together with ice; shake to chill. Strain into a double old-fashioned glass over a large ice cube. Garnish with an orange wheel and an extra dash of Angostura bitters over the top of the drink. Put the cinnamon stick in the drink and light the top end on fire so it sends sparks of spicy cinnamon aroma flying into the air. Serve and watch the lights go wild.

FROM THE VAULT: *An almond-based syrup with roots that date back to the eighteenth century, orgeat is a staple in many tropical drinks, like the Mai Tai. It's easy to make at home if you have almonds, sugar, and orange flower water, and it's even easier to buy online. Versions made by Liber & Co. and Small Hand Foods are especially delicious.*

This was the day I learned fire is hot.

Team Jacob

Team Jacob is perfect for occasions that call for swallowing your pride and dishing out an apology to an old flame. The wintry hot chocolate is spiked with a little bit of amaro to represent the bittersweet feelings that come with wishing you could go back and change the way a relationship played out. Mix up your favorite hot chocolate recipe, grab the whipped cream, turn around, and make it alright.

1-1/2 OUNCES AMARO

4 TO 5 OUNCES HOT CHOCOLATE

WHIPPED CREAM, FOR GARNISH

ORANGE PEEL

GRATED CINNAMON, FOR GARNISH

In your favorite mug, combine the hot chocolate and amaro. Top with whipped cream. Squeeze the orange peel over the top of the drink to express the oils, and discard the peel. Sprinkle a pinch of grated cinnamon over the top as a final flourish. Serve and toast to your Tay of choice.

FROM THE VAULT: *Let's say you're not an amaro fan—that's totally cool. You can spike hot chocolate with a bunch of different spirits, like vodka, peppermint schnapps, or mezcal. If your experiment doesn't work out, you can toss that version and try again.*

The Best Revenge

When faced with words that are like knives and swords and weapons used against you, the best revenge is living well. "Mean" was Tay's clapback to the time a harsh critic pointed out a flawed onstage moment with a loudspeaker in the media. In the same spirit, this cocktail is a delicious way to give haters the bird. We know how Taylor used to love drinking Diet Coke and vodka—leading snobs to grumble about her having bad taste—so this update is an opportunity to own it. A scoop of vanilla ice cream makes the finish extra sweet. You've got nobody to impress, so drink what you want and live your best life, critics be damned! All they're ever gonna be is mean.

1 SCOOP VANILLA
ICE CREAM

1-1/2 OUNCES VODKA

4 TO 5 OUNCES COLA

In a highball glass filled with ice about halfway up, combine the cola and vodka, followed by the ice cream and a straw. Take a big sip and forget all about that person who's a liar, pathetic, alone in life, and mean, and mean, and mean, and mean.

YOUR (N/A) VERSION: *Sure, you could just omit the vodka and have a regular old Coke float if that's how you're feeling in the moment, but for a spirit-free version of this drink that has a little more complexity, try throwing in an ounce and a half of zero-proof vodka, rum, or whiskey. Spiritless Kentucky 74 "bourbon" and Ritual Rum Alternative both taste especially delicious.*

TAYLOR SPEAKS

"No matter what you do, no matter how old you are, no matter what your job is, no matter what your place is in life, there's always going to be someone who's just mean to you. Dealing with that is all you can control about that situation, how you handle it. 'Mean' is about how I handle it, and sort of my mind set about this whole situation."

—HOLLER, 2023

Wonderstruck

Playful conversation starts, and a sparkling night of countering quick remarks leaves you wondering: Is it love at first sight? Or just wishful thinking? This enchanting drink captures all the wonderstruck feelings of a potential connection as it sings with the soft floral notes of violet liqueur—which also happens to make the drink the same color as the magnificent Eras Tour ball gown Taylor donned for this song. This drink is flawless. It's enchanting. Don't you let it go.

2 OUNCES	GIN (PREFERABLY HENDRICK'S)
1/2 OUNCE	CRÈME DE VIOLETTE LIQUEUR
3/4 OUNCE	FRESH LEMON JUICE
1/2 OUNCE	SIMPLE SYRUP (PAGE 25)
1 DASH	PEYCHAUD'S BITTERS
	PURPLE EDIBLE GLITTER, FOR SHIMMER (OPTIONAL)
3 OUNCES	CLUB SODA
	EDIBLE FLOWERS, FOR GARNISH

Pour the club soda into a Collins glass three-quarters full of ice; set aside. In a shaker tin, combine the edible glitter (if using), Peychaud's bitters, simple syrup, lemon juice, crème de violette, and gin. Add ice and shake to chill, then strain into the prepared Collins glass. Garnish with the prettiest edible flowers you can find and serve, feeling the blush all the way home.

FROM THE VAULT: *Known primarily for its role in the Aviation cocktail, crème de violette is a low-proof liqueur made with violet flowers, which historically symbolize secret love. The versions made by Rothman & Winter and Giffard are bar-quality options. The former is made only with brandy and fruit (no vanilla, which other recipes may contain). If floral liqueurs are not your thing, you could use a fruit liqueur in its place, like crème de cassis or crème de mûre.*

For You

Taylor has gifted us with so much magic over the years, infusing passion into everything she does. When she wrote "Long Live" as a dedication to her fans, bandmates, and production team, she asked us to remember this moment in the back of our minds. This sparkling low-ABV cocktail is a great way to do just that. As a toast to all of us, the drink is anchored by a passion fruit liqueur with flavor so vibrant it could move mountains. For the heroes, kings, queens, and Swifties everywhere—all the kingdom lights shine for us. We will be remembered.

1 OUNCE	CHINOLA PASSION FRUIT LIQUEUR
1 DASH	ANGOSTURA BITTERS
4 OUNCES	CHAMPAGNE OR SPARKLING WINE
	LEMON PEEL, FOR GARNISH

In a double old-fashioned glass over one large ice cube, combine the Champagne or sparkling wine with the Angostura bitters and passion fruit liqueur. Stir briefly to combine. Squeeze the lemon peel over the top of the drink to express the oils, and place the peel in the glass as a garnish. Serve and toast to all the magic we made.

TAYLOR SPEAKS

"Musically and lyrically, Red resembled a heartbroken person. . . . It was all over the place, a fractured mosaic of feelings that somehow all fit together in the end. Happy, free, confused, lonely, devastated, euphoric, wild, and tortured by memories past."

—NME, 2021

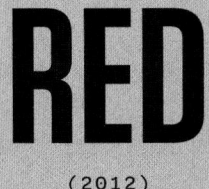

RED

(2012)

The subtle threads of pop that wove through *Speak Now* get amplified in Taylor's *Red* era, where she pointedly explores themes of heartbreak and all the highs and lows that come with it. The album shows her on the precipice of adulthood as she starts experimenting with different musical styles, too—for example, in songs like "I Knew You Were Trouble," heavy bass and electronics give the dance jam a clubby vibe, while "22" is a lighthearted party anthem secretly dedicated to her BFFs. Her aesthetic during this time also evolved to match the more electric energy of the album, as she most notably ditched her classic curls in favor of a short fringe. The drinks in this era range in style from big, bold stirred cocktails for songs like "Red" to refreshing, slightly sassy ones for "We Are Never Ever Getting Back Together." Like the album itself, the collection of recipes has quite a few little surprises—like the addition of cherries to the mojito variation on page 72—plus a few ingredients that balance youthful exuberance with mature self-reflection, like Jägermeister in Cold Hard Ground (page 68) and coffee liqueur in F*ck the Patriarchy (page 71).

★ *Blondie's influence bled into TV and film during this era, with guest appearances on shows like* New Girl *and movies like* The Giver. *She was also nominated for best original song for "Sweeter Than Fiction" from the* One Chance *soundtrack, and "I Knew You Were Trouble" earned a spotlight on the popular TV show* Glee.

★ Red *surpassed a Beatles record, as an album that spent more than six weeks at No. 1 on the Billboard 200.*

★ *Many of the songs on the album were likely written about her relationship with Jake Gyllenhaal, but her headline-grabbing relationship at the time was with Harry Styles.*

MASERATI NEGRONI

What better way to kick-start the *Red* era than with the reddest cocktail of all time? Classically made with gin, sweet vermouth, and Campari, the Negroni is a super flexible drink that tastes even better with a few upgrades. In this case, crème de cacao and orange bitters step in as companions to Punt e Mes, a hybrid vermouth-amaro that amps up the old standby to Maserati status. Sweet vermouth sticks around for the party, but to get the best results, use a high-quality brand, like Cocchi vermouth di Tornio or Carpano Antica, to keep the cocktail nice and luxe. Big, bold, bittersweet: It's like a love so strong it practically sizzles. Memorize it, like the words to your old favorite song.

1 OUNCE	GIN
3/4 OUNCE	PUNT E MES
3/4 OUNCE	SWEET VERMOUTH
1/2 OUNCE	CAMPARI
1	BARSPOON CRÈME DE CACAO
1 DASH	ORANGE BITTERS (PREFERABLY SCRAPPY'S)
1 DASH	ANGOSTURA COCOA BITTERS
	ORANGE PEEL, FOR GARNISH

In a mixing glass, combine the two types of bitters, crème de cacao, Campari, sweet vermouth, Punt e Mes, and gin with ice. Stir until chilled. Strain into a double old-fashioned glass over one large ice cube or sphere. Squeeze the orange peel over the top of the drink to express the oils, and discard the peel. Serve to keep the blues and dark grays at bay.

FROM THE VAULT: *Punt e Mes is an Italian vermouth with the same opulence as a good sweet vermouth, but with a bracing backbone of bitterness that makes it a complex option for using in drinks like a Manhattan or Negroni. For those inclined towards bitter flavors, it tastes great on the rocks as well. If you can't find Punt e Mes, you can use sweet vermouth instead, but the drink won't have as much complexity.*

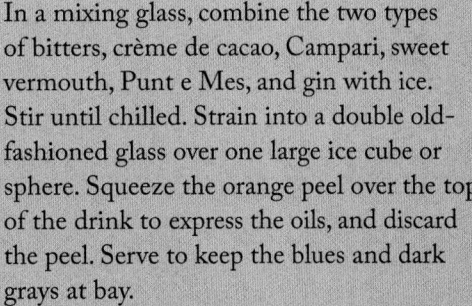

COLD HARD GROUND

Have you ever heard of a Jäger-based margarita? Sounds like trouble, right? There is no getting away from the fact that this might be a bad idea, but we're going to do it anyway. Soon you'll see the joke's on you—the way the dried orange and clove notes of the German herbal liqueur meld with vegetal blanco tequila is pleasantly surprising, and the luxe pomegranate flavor from the grenadine flies the drink to places it's never been. Trouble? Yep. Shame? Nah. Bottoms up!

1-1/2 OUNCES JÄGERMEISTER

1/2 OUNCE BLANCO TEQUILA

3/4 OUNCE FRESH LIME JUICE

1/4 OUNCE GRENADINE (PAGE 28)

2 DASHES ORANGE BITTERS
(PREFERABLY SCRAPPY'S)

ORANGE PEEL,
FOR GARNISH

In a shaker tin with ice, combine the orange bitters with the grenadine, lime juice, tequila, and Jägermeister. Shake to chill, then strain into a coupe glass. Squeeze the orange peel over the top of the drink to express the oils, then discard the peel. Serve and remember when they saw you dancing.

YOUR (N/A) VERSION: *Made with a hemp base and spiced with sage, ginger, saffron, orange peels, and other botanicals, The Pathfinder is an excellent N/A amaro option for this drink. The flavor is not identical to Jäger, but it's a real banger in its own right. Don't forget to also grab orange bitters from All The Bitters and sub in your favorite tequila alternative, too— Almave Ámbar is a great call because its honeyed orange notes pair well with the saffron and ginger of The Pathfinder. You can keep the same measurements for all of the ingredients in the drink, except for the grenadine—increase that to a ½ ounce pour to bring sweetness to the mix.*

F*CK THE PATRIARCHY

Nothing's getting lost in translation in this boozy take on one of the coffee orders that made headlines for Taylor: the maple latte. With a poignant punch of whiskey in the mix, it's the ultimate cold comfort for reflecting on times both good and bad. It's especially delicious when autumn leaves are falling down outside like pieces falling into place, or to accompany the first snow of the season, when it's time to pull out your favorite scarf. The perfect balance of creamy, boozy, and bitter, the flavor will linger with you long after the last sip.

1-1/2 OUNCES BOURBON

1/2 OUNCE RYE WHISKEY

1/2 OUNCE COFFEE LIQUEUR

3/4 OUNCE HALF-AND-HALF

1/2 OUNCE MAPLE SYRUP

1 DASH ORANGE BITTERS
(PREFERABLY SCRAPPY'S)

ORANGE PEEL,
FOR GARNISH

In a shaker tin with ice, combine the orange bitters, maple syrup, half-and-half, coffee liqueur, rye whiskey, and bourbon. Shake to chill. Strain into a double old-fashioned glass over one large ice cube. Squeeze the orange peel over the top of the drink to express the oils, and discard the peel. Serve and ask yourself: How'd that make you feel?

MOJITO 22

Who didn't love a good mojito in their twenties? Taylor certainly did, and rightfully so: Despite having come in and out of fashion over the years, this classic cocktail tastes great with breakfast at midnight, or while you're making fun of your exes. It's versatile, too—in this version, a few pops of bright cherry come into the mix to help punch up the energy needed for a carefree night on the town. It's happy, free, confused, and lonely at the same time. Miserable and magical. Forget about the heartbreak. Dance like you're 22!

2 OUNCES	WHITE RUM (PREFERABLY PLANTERAY 3 STAR)
3/4 OUNCE	FRESH LIME JUICE
1/4 OUNCE	LUXARDO MARASCHINO CHERRY SYRUP (FROM THE JAR OF CHERRIES)
1/4 OUNCE	SIMPLE SYRUP (PAGE 25)
3	LUXARDO MARASCHINO CHERRIES
3	SPRIGS MINT
3 OUNCES	CLUB SODA
1	BOUQUET OF MINT, FOR GARNISH

Fill a Collins glass three-quarters full with ice and add the club soda and set aside. Add the mint sprigs and cherries to a shaker tin and muddle together until the cherries are nice and pummeled. Add the simple syrup, cherry syrup, lime juice, and white rum. Add ice and shake to chill. Strain into the prepared Collins glass and garnish with the mint bouquet. Serve and toast to #DrunkTaylor (and know that after two, you may turn into a wizard).

TAYLOR SPEAKS

"To me, the red emotions are the most powerful ones on the good side and the bad side—affection and infatuation and love and warmth, and on the other side you have anger, jealousy, frustration, miscommunication, all of those horrible ones. I think no matter what side you are on, you are feeling the most amount of emotion you could possibly feel, if you're feeling a red emotion. I've always referred to those kinds of relationships as red relationships."
—SIRIUSXM, 2012

TRACK "We Are Never Ever
Getting Back Together"

DRINK A blackberry gimlet
for when it's time to
show your too-cool ex
the door

NEVER SAY NEVER

Life is so much more delicious when you stop caring about what other people think. That's just what Taylor did when she penned this defiant breakup track for one of her more famous ex-boyfriends. For the guy who thinks indie records are superior to pop ones, writing one of the most catchy earworm tracks of all time is one hell of a way to prove you'll never, ever, ever, ever, get back together. Had enough? Toast to that sassy sentiment with this delectable blackberry and mint version of the gimlet.

2 OUNCES	GIN
3/4 OUNCE	FRESH LIME JUICE
3/4 OUNCE	SIMPLE SYRUP (PAGE 25)
8	BLACKBERRIES
	BOUQUET OF MINT, FOR GARNISH

In a shaker tin, briefly muddle 5 of the blackberries to extract some of the juice. Add the simple syrup, lime juice, and gin, plus ice. Shake to chill and double-strain into a coupe glass: Hold a fine-mesh strainer underneath the Hawthorne strainer as you strain. Garnish with 3 blackberries skewered on a cocktail pick, with several sprigs of mint stuck into the top of each berry. Serve with a little ooh-ooh-ooh-ooh-ooh.

YOUR (N/A) VERSION: *This time, I'm telling you, I'm telling you: Blackberries, lime, and mint paint such a beautiful canvas for this cocktail that they work with almost any base spirit you fancy. When this is it, you've had enough (booze), you can experiment with your favorite N/A gins, whiskeys, or vodkas to see what combo tastes best to you. If you need a rec, Monday Zero gin has a rebellious backbone that stands up nicely to the berries, so that's a solid place to start.*

FRESH START

Channeling those Wednesday café vibes, where fresh starts and new beginnings spark, this cocktail is a mash-up of an espresso-tonic and an Americano cocktail (Campari, sweet vermouth, and soda). With a dose of revitalizing coffee, snappy brightness from the tonic water, and blooming orange notes from the bitters and Campari, it's a delicious way to let go of the idea that all love ever does is break and burn. With each sip, watch how it can begin again.

1 OUNCE COFFEE LIQUEUR
(PREFERABLY KAHLÚA)

1 OUNCE CAMPARI

2 DASHES ORANGE BITTERS
(PREFERABLY
SCRAPPY'S)

4 TO 5 OUNCES TONIC WATER
(PREFERABLY
FEVER-TREE)

ORANGE PEEL,
FOR GARNISH

Fill an old-fashioned glass three-quarters full with ice, and add 4 ounces of the tonic water. Add the orange bitters, Campari, and coffee liqueur. Give it a stir to combine the ingredients, and taste. If the flavor is too concentrated, add more tonic water. Squeeze the orange peel over the top of the drink to express the oils and place the peel in the glass as a garnish. Serve and feel free to wear heels now.

1989

(2014)

Titled after the year she was born, *1989* signaled Taylor's unapologetic arrival into the pop music realm, as she left all traces of her country days behind and fully embraced her place in the industry as a global tour de force. She moved to NYC, shifted her style fully from princess to pop star, and turned up the volume on her independence with songs like "Shake It Off" and "Wildest Dreams." To celebrate the vibrancy of her success during this time, the drinks in this chapter are bursting with big, bold flavors and shimmery sentiments. Get ready to celebrate her arrival in the Big Apple with a spin on the iconic Cosmo (page 80), shake off bad energy with a wicked shot to accompany "Bad Blood" (page 88), or get lost in the ethereal magic of "This Love" with a clever cover of the Corpse Reviver #2 (page 92).

★ *The media attention on the details of her friendships and relationships increased dramatically during this time, highlighting her splashy feud with Kanye West and Kim Kardashian and her famously tight-knit squad of friends—many of whom, including Selena Gomez, HAIM, and Lorde, showed up for surprise guest appearances during the 1989 world tour.*

★ *When 1989 won Album of the Year at the Grammys, it marked the first time a woman had won this award twice; she was also named Woman of the Year by Billboard magazine for the second time.*

★ *She launched "secret sessions" during this time, where she invites fans to listen to albums and discuss the lyrics and themes before they officially drop.*

LIGHTS ARE SO BRIGHT

We begin our story in New York, where the classic Cosmopolitan was invented. It's such a perfect cocktail—smart, sassy, and ambitious—that it's no surprise Queen Taylor has her own favorite version. The Tay-Tini, made with vodka, orange liqueur, cranberry, lemon, and peach schnapps, is a delicious spin on the original Cosmo. In the same spirit, this riff on her recipe welcomes rich pomegranate flavor to the glass via a dose of grenadine, and shimmers bright as NYC lights with edible glitter. It's so delicious, it'll have you dancing to this beat all night long.

1-1/2 OUNCES VODKA

1/2 OUNCE GIN

1/2 OUNCE CRANBERRY JUICE

3/4 OUNCE FRESH LEMON JUICE

1/2 OUNCE GRENADINE (PAGE 28)

1 BARSPOON PEACH SCHNAPPS (OPTIONAL)

PINK EDIBLE GLITTER (OPTIONAL)

LEMON TWIST, FOR GARNISH

In a shaker tin, combine the edible glitter (if using), peach schnapps (if using), grenadine, lemon and cranberry juices, gin, and vodka. Add ice and shake to chill. Strain into a martini glass and garnish by resting the lemon twist on the rim of the glass. Serve it right away: It's been waiting for you!

YOUR (N/A) VERSION: *Like any true love, this booze-less Cosmo will drive you crazy. To make one, omit the vodka and gin, then sub in two full ounces of spirit-free gin. Seedlip Grove 42 has a searingly bright citrusy personality that lifts the grenadine and matches the intensity of the cranberry juice, but it can be a touch demure against such bold companions, so if you go this route, also increase the grenadine to a ¾ ounce, so the drink stays so bright (but never blinding).*

JAMES DEAN DAYDREAM

What time is it, Taylor? It's martini time! Like the classic white T-shirt and the perfect shade of red lipstick, gin and vermouth were simply made for each other—a combo that hits the right notes every time. This cocktail is the perfect pregame sipper for meeting up with that special someone— the one who always looks at you with a sparkle in their eye. It's also got that red cherry classic thing that you like—a sweet little red kiss at the bottom of the glass.

1-1/2 OUNCES GIN (PREFERABLY FORDS)

1-1/2 OUNCES DOLIN BLANC VERMOUTH

1 BARSPOON LUXARDO MARASCHINO LIQUEUR

1 BARSPOON SIMPLE SYRUP (PAGE 25)

LUXARDO MARASCHINO CHERRY, FOR GARNISH

Fill a mixing glass with ice, then add the simple syrup, maraschino liqueur, blanc vermouth, and gin. Stir to chill. Put the Luxardo maraschino cherry at the bottom of a Nick and Nora glass, then strain the cocktail over the cherry. Serve it up and they'll come back every time.

FROM THE VAULT: *There are a lot of cherry liqueurs on the market, but the one made by Luxardo is the best option for this cocktail—it has a sophistication that's second to none. The full-size bottles can be a little pricey, but many liquor stores also sell half-size versions. It's an ingredient you might only use a barspoon of here and there, so the investment will last you a long time—you can also use it to make the recipes on pages 158 and 162—but if you really don't want to invest in a bottle, you can use some of the syrup from the cherries to sweeten this cocktail instead. The color will change, but it'll still taste like a cherry martini.*

IN SCREAMING COLOR

Sometimes it takes losing someone else to find yourself, but seeing the forest for the trees can be almost impossible when you're in the thick of a relationship. In those moments you've gotta figure out how to get through the hard times before you can fly on your own again. In this version of the Paper Plane—a modern classic made with bourbon, amaro, Aperol, and lemon—a bit of honey and club soda are added to take the drink to new heights. Sipping one feels like rising above the fray, leaving the darkness behind, and finding out the monsters turned out to be just trees. Are we in the clear yet? In the clear yet? Good.

3/4 OUNCE WHISKEY

3/4 OUNCE APEROL

3/4 OUNCE AMARO

3/4 OUNCE FRESH LEMON JUICE

1/4 OUNCE HONEY SYRUP
(PAGE 26)

3 TO 4 OUNCES CLUB SODA

LEMON TWIST,
FOR GARNISH

Place 4 or 5 ice cubes in a Collins glass and add the club soda; set aside. In a shaker tin, combine the honey syrup, lemon juice, amaro, Aperol, and whiskey. Add ice and shake to chill. Strain the cocktail into the prepared Collins glass and garnish by placing the lemon twist on the edge of the glass. Serve and set yourself free.

TAYLOR SPEAKS

"I am in love with catchy melodies and hooks that are stuck in your head for days, and ideally weeks, and even months. I really love it when I hear a song, and all of a sudden, my next two weeks are spent trying to figure out how to get that song out of my head."
—TIME, 2014

MY KIND OF REBELLION

In a 2009 interview with *Rolling Stone,* Taylor said, "Rebellion is what you make of it," and in the years since, it's clear her kind of rebellion is doing her own thing in spite of the haters and the players, the fakers, and the dirty, dirty cheats. If you're ready to embrace the same spirit and set off the Richter scale, this cocktail is for you. You can personalize this drink with whatever base spirit you want, as it tastes great with gin, whiskey, brandy, vodka, or even alcohol-free. It just needs a nice, long shake, shake, shake to get the honey into the mix. Put on your dancing shoes and know it's gonna be alright.

2 OUNCES   YOUR SPIRIT OF CHOICE

3/4 OUNCE   FRESH LEMON JUICE

1/2 OUNCE   HONEY SYRUP (PAGE 26)

2 DASHES   ORANGE BITTERS
            (PREFERABLY SCRAPPY'S)

In a shaker tin, combine the orange bitters with the honey syrup, lemon juice, and spirit of choice. Add ice, then shake to chill. Once it feels cold to the touch, open the shaker and strain the cocktail into an old-fashioned glass over fresh ice. Serve, and keep cruisin'.

YOUR (N/A) VERSION: *A myriad of booze-free spirits would work well in this recipe, in the event you'd prefer a zero-buzz version. Seedlip Garden 108 brings a light rosemary and spearmint personality to the drink; Spiritless Kentucky 74 serves as a whiskey alternative with robust oak notes; Ritual "rum" bolsters the drink with caramel and sugarcane flavors; and for an outside-the-box option, Three Spirit Livener adds an invigorating fruity character to the drink, with adaptogenic berries, Amazonian holly, and watermelon. Just remember to use All the Bitters orange bitters instead of booze-fueled ones, and you're good to go!*

BUUUURN!

When mad love turns into bad blood (hey!), there's only one solution: It's time for shots. Betrayal from a wolf in friend's clothing is a different kind of heartbreak, so this combo features an abnormal amount of Angostura bitters—like throwing extra salt in the wound. The ingredient is normally only used sparingly, in dashes, but when poured by the ounce it packs a cold-blooded punch of baking-spice burn.

1 OUNCE   ANGOSTURA BITTERS

1 OUNCE   CAMPARI

Combine the Campari and Angostura bitters in a shaker tin with ice and shake to chill. Strain into your favorite shot glass. Serve and think about the good times.

FROM THE VAULT: *If you want to make enough for a group, just multiply the quantities based on the number of people drinking.*

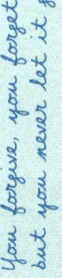

You forgive, you forget, but you never let it go.

RED LIPS AND ROSY CHEEKS

Forbidden love shouldn't taste this good, but heaven help us, the strawberries in this Aperol spritz make the classic cocktail so handsome it'll land in your wildest dreams. A tiny squeeze of lemon juice isn't typical in this drink, but the kiss of citrus will help balance out its juicy sweetness without adding flavor, so give that a whirl anyway—no one has to know. Mix one up next time you're standing in a nice dress staring at the sunset, babe.

3 OUNCES SPARKLING ROSÉ WINE

1-1/2 OUNCES CLUB SODA

1 BARSPOON FRESH LEMON JUICE

2 OUNCES APEROL

4 FRESH STRAWBERRIES

Slice 3 of the strawberries in half. In a shaker tin, muddle the sliced strawberries with the Aperol, then add the lemon juice and ice, and shake to chill. Set aside. Add ice cubes to a wine or spritz glass, then add the sparkling rosé and the club soda. Double-strain the strawberry Aperol mixture into the prepared glass: Hold a fine-mesh strainer underneath the Hawthorne strainer as you strain. Stir to combine all the ingredients. Make a slice into the remaining strawberry and set it on the rim to garnish. Serve and let its memory follow you around.

YOUR (N/A) VERSION: *For a memorable zero-proof version of this cocktail, a de-alcoholized sparkling rosé, such as the signature sparkling Chardonnay-Merlot blend from Maison Chavin, pairs swimmingly with Lapo's Non-Alcoholic Aperitivo or Lyre's Italian Orange non-alcoholic spirit.*

SINKING SHIPS

Taylor's lyricism in "This Love" is so captivating—the story of being lost at sea and coming back safely, of a love that comes back around revitalized, resurrected—it's downright hypnotic. This cover of the classic Corpse Reviver #2, with honeyed, herbal green Chartreuse, ghostly absinthe, and just a hint of minerality from the mezcal, captures the celestial vibes of the song. The finish goes on and on, on and on. . . .

3/4 OUNCE   MEZCAL (PREFERABLY DEL MAGUEY VIDA)

3/4 OUNCE   DOLIN BLANC VERMOUTH

3/4 OUNCE   GREEN CHARTREUSE

3/4 OUNCE   FRESH LIME JUICE

1/4 OUNCE   ABSINTHE

1 DASH   ORANGE BITTERS (PREFERABLY SCRAPPY'S)

ORANGE PEEL, FOR GARNISH

In a shaker tin, combine the orange bitters, absinthe, lime juice, green Chartreuse, blanc vermouth, and mezcal. Add ice and shake to chill, then strain into a coupe glass. Squeeze the orange peel over the top of the drink to express the oils and discard the peel. Serve and feel alive, back from the dead.

NOT-SO-STYLISH ENDING

Was it over then? Is it over now? Flash-forward to three hundred takeout coffees later: No matter what happens with your significant other in the long run, this smoldering stirred cocktail will still be there for you. With a hefty pour of whiskey, a stinging bite of coffee liqueur, and a little sweet vermouth to smooth out the rough edges, it's an ideal drink for when unresolved questions and whispered sighs from a great love still linger.

1-1/2 OUNCES SCOTCH

1/2 OUNCE RYE WHISKEY

1/2 OUNCE COFFEE LIQUEUR
(PREFERABLY KAHLÚA)

1/2 OUNCE SWEET VERMOUTH

3 DASHES ORANGE BITTERS
(PREFERABLY SCRAPPY'S)

ORANGE PEEL,
FOR GARNISH

In a mixing glass, combine the orange bitters, sweet vermouth, coffee liqueur, rye whiskey, and Scotch. Add ice and stir to chill. Strain into a double old-fashioned glass over a large ice cube. Squeeze the orange peel over the top of the drink to express the oils, and place the peel in the glass as a garnish. Serve and say the one thing you've been wanting.

Reputation

(2017)

With *Reputation*, Taylor's sound took a striking turn away from the bubbly synth pop of *1989*, moving towards a more edgy and experimental style marked by bombastic electronic and industrial sounds. Many of the songs—"Don't Blame Me" and "Look What You Made Me Do" especially—symbolically left her "girl next door" image in the dust as she worked to reclaim her narrative from the vicious tabloid headlines and public scrutiny that happened in the wake of her feud with Kanye West and Kim Kardashian. (As is her style, there are some tender moments of vulnerability baked into the mix too, via tracks like "Delicate.") The cocktails in this group are a mix of drinks with a serious attitude—daring, unapologetic, spicy cocktails that channel this electrifying energy, like Take Us to Church (page 101) and Rose from the Dead (page 105)—plus a few that ride the waves of soft longing, like Forevermore (page 106).

★ *As usual, Swift dominated the charts with this album, which also won awards at the Billboard Music Awards, MTV Video Music Awards, and American Music Awards.*

★ *During the lifespan of* Reputation, *Blondie shifted her usual marketing tactics and largely stayed out of the spotlight, refusing interviews for about a year after the album released.*

★ *In 2017, she won a high-profile sexual assault case against radio DJ David Mueller, who had inappropriately groped her during a meet-and-greet event, months before the #MeToo reckoning swept the land.*

Let the Games Begin

T-Swift mentions drinks in a lot of her songs—usually old-fashioneds and bottles of wine and slugs of whiskey—and in this jam, she mentions the island breeze, a fruity cocktail made with coconut rum, pineapple, cranberry, and peach schnapps. Yet with its provocative beats and seriously sassy attitude, "... Ready For It?" begs for a cocktail with a sexier tone than the original. See how this is gonna go? No one has to know. As a perfect precursor to midnight hookups, this tropical fever dream starts with sultry rum and honey "bass" notes and ends with a wicked snake bite of amaro and bitters. Turn the lights down low, mix one up, and let the games begin.

2 OUNCES	AGED RUM (PREFERABLY PLANTERAY 5-YEAR)
1 OUNCE	PINEAPPLE JUICE
3/4 OUNCE	FRESH LEMON JUICE
1/2 OUNCE	AMARO (OPTIONAL)
3/4 OUNCE	HONEY SYRUP (PAGE 26)
1 DASH	ANGOSTURA BITTERS
	PINEAPPLE LEAF, FOR GARNISH

In a shaker tin, combine the Angostura bitters, honey syrup, amaro (if using), lemon juice, pineapple juice, and aged rum. Add ice and shake to chill. Strain into a tropical mug over fresh ice and garnish with the pineapple leaf. Take your time serving.

YOUR (N/A) VERSION: *As a Burton to this Taylor, this drink tastes just as good with zero-proof ingredients, so if you're not drinking for whatever reason, queue up your best alternatives and get mixing! The Pathfinder works splendidly in place of traditional amaro, and for a straightforward rum swap, reach for Ritual "rum." Three Spirit Nightcap also works as a quirky rum option—the booze-less elixir has notes of lemon balm, Mosaic hops, and valerian, which makes it resemble a spiced rum.*

Take Us to Church

Lord save us all, this drink will bring you to the darkest little paradise. To capture the same femme fatale vibes Tay infuses into the verses and chorus of "Don't Blame Me," this spicy mezcal margarita tastes unexpectedly dark and twisty, thanks to the use of chipotle-cacao bitters. If you've been breaking hearts for a long time, join the line at the confessional booth, because this one's worth keeping around for the rest of your life.

1 OUNCE   MEZCAL (PREFERABLY DEL MAGUEY VIDA)

1 OUNCE   BLANCO TEQUILA

3/4 OUNCE   FRESH LIME JUICE

3/4 OUNCE   SIMPLE SYRUP (PAGE 25)

2 DASHES   BITTERCUBE CHIPOTLE-CACAO BITTERS

LIME WEDGE & SMOKED SALT, FOR THE RIM

Prepare an old-fashioned glass by running the lime wedge around half of the rim then coating the wet rim with smoked salt. In a shaker tin, combine the chipotle-cacao bitters with the syrup, lime juice, tequila, and mezcal. Add ice and shake to chill. Strain into the glass over 4 or 5 ice cubes. Serve and let it make you feel crazy. If it doesn't, you ain't doin' it right.

YOUR (N/A) VERSION: *If you're ready to cross the line, a simple substitution of alcohol-free mezcal and booze-less tequila make this smoldering sensation more inclusive for anyone who's not drinking. The agave options from A Cut Above gel together well, if you're looking for a good place to begin. If you want to only use one bottle instead of two, try the Almave Blanco, which is made with real blue agave, for best results. Just don't forget to omit the bitters entirely if 100 percent booze-free is the goal, because they will add a very small amount of alcohol to the drink.*

TRACK *"Delicate"*   DRINK *A cool-headed highball for breaking through barriers*

1, 2, 3, Let's Go B*tch

As at home in a fancy cocktail bar as it would be in a dive bar on NYC's East Side, this simple highball looks pretty and delicate but it is nothing short of totally savage. It's perfect for situations when you need a little sip of courage to get past the "Is it cool I said all that?" moment. No promises that you'll get past the delicate conversations unscathed, babe, but you can make this drink in the meantime.

1-1/2 OUNCES GIN (PREFERABLY FORD'S)

3/4 OUNCE DOLIN BLANC VERMOUTH

3 OUNCES TONIC WATER (PREFERABLY FEVER-TREE)

ROSEMARY SPRIG, FOR GARNISH

In a highball glass, combine the tonic water and 4 or 5 ice cubes; set aside. In a mixing glass, combine the blanc vermouth and gin with more ice. Stir to chill, then strain the cold cocktail into the prepared highball glass and garnish with the rosemary sprig. Serve, and honey, you won't want to share.

TAYLOR SPEAKS

"At the very beginning of the album I was pretty proud of coining the term, 'There will be no explanation. There will just be Reputation.' . . . And so that was what I decided was going to be the album. And I stuck with it. I didn't go back on it. I didn't try to explain the album because I didn't feel that I owed that to anyone. There was a lot that happened over a couple of years that made me feel really, really terrible. And I didn't feel like expressing that to them. I didn't feel like talking about it. I just felt like making music, then going out on the road and doing a stadium tour and doing everything I could for my fans."

—APPLE MUSIC INTERVIEW WITH ZANE LOWE, 2019

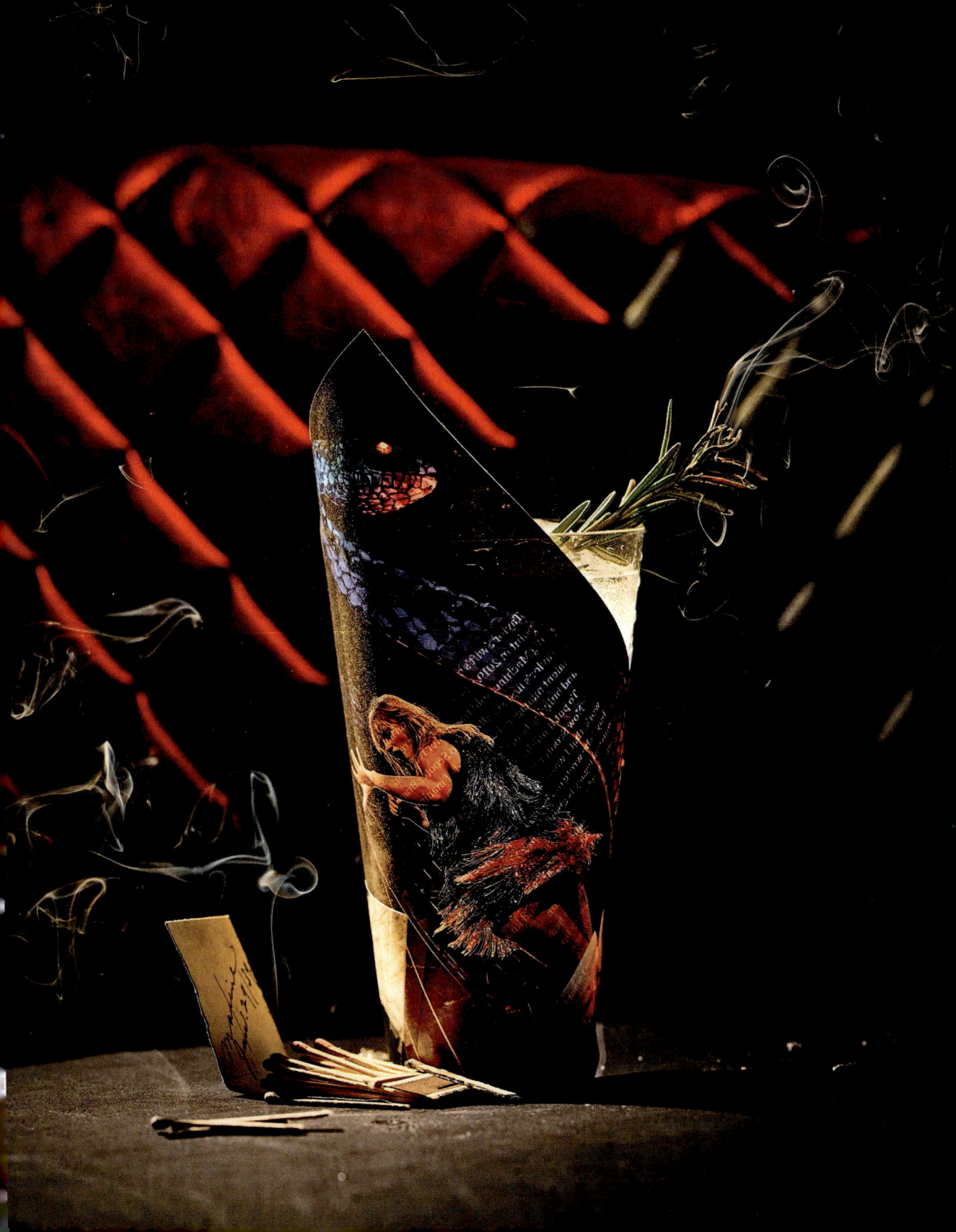

Rose from the Dead

I'm sorry, but the old zombie can't come to the phone right now. Why? Oh, 'cause it's dead. There's nothing wrong with the OG tiki drink, but in the spirit of T-Swizzle staging a comeback with this noir club track, let's make space for something new to rise up, just in the nick of time. This update is bolstered by an unabashed one-two punch of tequila and rum, making it smarter, harder, and more delicious than the original.

1 OUNCE	REPOSADO TEQUILA
1 OUNCE	AGED RUM
3/4 OUNCE	FRESH LIME JUICE
1/2 OUNCE	CINNAMON SYRUP (PAGE 27)
1/4 OUNCE	GRENADINE (PAGE 28)
1 DASH	ANGOSTURA BITTERS
1 TO 2 OUNCES	ABSINTHE, TO RINSE THE GLASS
	BOUQUET OF MINT, FOR GARNISH

Prepare an old-fashioned glass: Fill it with crushed ice, add the absinthe, and stir until absinthe coats the interior of the glass; set aside. In a shaker tin, combine the Angostura bitters, grenadine, cinnamon syrup, lime juice, aged rum, and reposado tequila. Add ice and shake to chill. Set aside. Pour the crushed ice and absinthe out of the old-fashioned glass (into the sink), angling the glass as you do this so the absinthe continues to coat the interior of the glass on its way out. Refill the glass with fresh crushed ice and strain the prepared cocktail into the glass. Garnish with the mint bouquet. Serve and there will be no further explanation, just reputation.

YOUR (N/A) VERSION: *Omit the absinthe as you build the rest of the drink with alcohol-free alternatives. The combo of Almave Ámbar and Three Spirit Nightcap make it one that'll star in your bad dreams with spectacular spice and vanilla notes, but you can experiment with other favorites to find a combo that suits your palate. Check it once, check it twice, oh: For the bitters, try All The Bitter aromatic bitters—they are a workhorse sub for the classic Angostura.*

To Karyn and Taylor, two misunderstood souls who felt so understood by each other.

Forevermore

Reputation is known as one of Taylor's most searing albums, but there are a few under-the-radar tracks that lean into the softer, more sentimental side of her songwriting. "New Year's Day" is an especially touching, stripped-down ballad about cherishing the quiet, intimate moments with a loved one. As a toast to the ones who get our midnights and mornings after, this tender little brunch drink stars orange marmalade and Cocchi Americano — it's a memorable medley of warm spiced orange and brioche notes from the bubbly.

1-1/2 OUNCES COCCHI AMERICANO (OR LILLET BLANC)

3/4 OUNCE FRESH LEMON JUICE

1 TABLESPOON ORANGE MARMALADE

1 DASH ORANGE BITTERS (PREFERABLY. SCRAPPY'S)

3 OUNCES CHAMPAGNE OR SPARKLING WINE

LEMON TWIST, FOR GARNISH

Add the Champagne or sparkling wine to a flute (or coupe, if you fancy) and set aside. Combine the orange bitters, marmalade, lemon juice, and Cocchi Americano in a shaker tin. Give it a stir to loosen up the jam, then add ice and shake to chill. Double-strain the mixture into the prepared glass: Hold a fine-mesh strainer underneath the Hawthorne strainer as you strain. Garnish by placing the lemon twist on the rim of the glass. Serve and hold on to the memories.

Lover

(2019)

In a hard pivot away from the femme fatale Taylor portrayed in *Reputation,* the *Lover* era is her return to beaming optimism—a virtual explosion of rainbow pastels and peppy performances, laced with undertones of whimsical romance and self-empowerment. She also infused some tracks with political themes; songs like "You Need To Calm Down" are especially significant because they aligned Taylor with the LGBTQ+ community. (The music video is a smorgasbord of fun, with the cast of *Queer Eye,* Ellen DeGeneres, and RuPaul making guest appearances.) To keep pace with this vibe, the drinks in this chapter are (mostly) bright, fruity, and fun, from a blackberry Pimm's cup for summer sipping (page 110) to a trio of playful shots for three very special souls in Tay's life (page 118). It's impossible to not enjoy drinking along to this magnetic era.

★ *Lover is her first album released via Republic Records. Her previous six albums were on Big Machine Records. In 2019, talent manager Scooter Braun acquired Big Machine, including the rights to Taylor's previous work, which led to a very public feud and prompting her to re-record her entire oeuvre. Each re-release is dubbed Taylor's Version.*

★ *Many of the songs on this album are suspected to be about her then-boyfriend Joe Alwyn, including the title track, "Lover."*

★ *Netflix released the documentary Miss Americana in 2020—the film explores the highs and lows of Taylor's personal growth as a creative artist and political advocate for various causes as she recorded the Lover album.*

Fever Dream

Summer flings can be equal parts bright bouncy butterflies and the sharp pangs of wanting something more serious. But there's no need to go get drunk in the back of the car and cry like a baby coming home from the bar when there's a delicious antidote like this at your fingertips. The Pimm's cup is one of T-Swizzle's favorites, and in this version—it's cool, there are no rules—the low-ABV cocktail keeps many of its classic elements (think breezy cucumber, strawberries, mint, and ginger beer) with bitters and blackberries swooping in to cut right to the bone. Not the worst thing you've ever heard, right? Roll the dice for this delicious dichotomy—it's worth the risk.

2 OUNCES	PIMM'S NO. 1
1/2 OUNCE	VODKA OR GIN
1/2 OUNCE	FRESH LIME JUICE
1/4 OUNCE	DEMERARA SYRUP (PAGE 25)
1 DASH	ANGOSTURA BITTERS
3	SLICES CUCUMBER
5	BLACKBERRIES
2	STRAWBERRIES (OPTIONAL)
5 OUNCES	FEVER-TREE GINGER BEER
	BOUQUET OF MINT, FOR GARNISH
2	BLACKBERRIES, FOR GARNISH

Add crushed ice and the ginger beer to a Collins glass; set aside. In a shaker tin, combine the berries and cucumber slices with the Angostura bitters and the demerara syrup. Muddle to crush it all together. Add the lime juice, vodka or gin, Pimm's No. 1, and ice, and shake to chill. Double-strain into the prepared Collins glass: Hold a fine-mesh strainer underneath the Hawthorne strainer as you strain. Garnish with the mint bouquet, a few blackberries, and serve, grinning like a devil.

Forever and Ever

Is there a better song for slow dancing than "Lover"? With sugar and spice and everything nice, this cocktail brings timeless ingredients like brandy, port, and Bénédictine together in a dazzling haze. Mix one up for the person you love hanging out with on the couch, the one you save your dirtiest jokes for, the one you feel you can just be yourself with, forever and ever.

1 OUNCE COGNAC (PREFERABLY FERRAND 1840)

1-1/2 OUNCES TAWNY PORT

1/4 OUNCE BÉNÉDICTINE

1 DASH ANGOSTURA BITTERS

1 DASH ORANGE BITTERS (PREFERABLY SCRAPPY'S)

ORANGE PEEL, FOR GARNISH

In a mixing glass, combine the Angostura and orange bitters, Bénédictine, port, and Cognac together with ice and stir to chill. Strain into a double old-fashioned glass over one large ice cube. Squeeze the orange peel over the top of the drink to express the oils, and place the peel in the glass as a garnish. Save a seat for your lover and serve.

FROM THE VAULT: *If you're leaving the Christmas lights up until January, use tangerine or clementine peels instead of orange for a little extra cheer.*

Paper Cut Stings

One of the most underrated tracks on *Lover*, "Death By A Thousand Cuts" is the story of a great love—one for the ages—that comes to an end after a long series of tiny problems adds up to something insurmountable. If you can't pretend it's okay when it's not, this minty daiquiri-inspired cocktail tastes like coming up for fresh air, with pine and clove notes brightened up with zesty lime juice.

2 OUNCES   WHITE RUM (PREFERABLY PLANTERAY 3 STAR)

1/4 OUNCE   GREEN CHARTREUSE

3/4 OUNCE   FRESH LIME JUICE

3/4 OUNCE   SIMPLE SYRUP (PAGE 25)

MINT SPRIG, FOR GARNISH

In a shaker tin, combine the syrup with the lime juice, green Chartreuse, and white rum. Add ice and shake hard to chill. Strain into a martini glass and garnish with the mint sprig. Serve and take the long way home.

TAYLOR SPEAKS

"Female artists in music have dominated this decade in growth, streaming, record and ticket sales, and critical acclaim. So why are we doing so well? Because we have to grow fast. We have to work this hard, we have to prove that we deserve this, and we have to top our last achievements. Women in music, on stage or behind the scenes, are not allowed to coast. We are held at a higher, sometimes impossible-feeling standard. And it seems that my fellow female artists have taken this challenge and they have accepted it." —WOMAN OF THE DECADE AWARD SPEECH AT BILLBOARD'S WOMEN IN MUSIC, 2019

Snakes and Stones

"You're taking shots at me like it's Patrón" is one of Swift's most glorious zingers of the *Lover* era, but it's her fantastical blender concoction from the music video for "You Need To Calm Down" that inspired this fun frozé recipe. Cotton candy vodka, if you can find it, makes this cocktail seriously extra, but you could experiment with whatever flavor you prefer. The same goes for the syrup—if you want to use strawberry or blackberry, it'll still taste deliciously powerful. When the trolls start trollin', it's time to bust out the blender and remind everyone: Why be mad when you could be GLAAD?

1-1/2 OUNCES VODKA (PREFERABLY COTTON CANDY FLAVOR)

6 OUNCES ROSÉ WINE

2 OUNCES RASPBERRY SYRUP

2 DASHES PEYCHAUD'S BITTERS

2 DASHES GRAPEFRUIT BITTERS

LEMON TWIST, FOR GARNISH

Add 1 cup of crushed ice to a blender, followed by the Peychaud's and grapefruit bitters, raspberry syrup, rosé, and vodka. Blend until smooth. Pour into a martini glass and garnish with the lemon twist perched on the rim of the glass. Serve and get your crown.

Childless Cat Lady

Taylor's cats are the light of her life, and because all three of them make an appearance in the music video for this collab with Brendon Urie of Panic! At The Disco, it's only fitting we strike up the band with one, two, three shots for all the saber-toothed tiger cubs, princesses of Meowtown, and unicorn kitty cats. Because each cat is one of a kind—and that's the fun of them—each shot has a different personality, too. The Meredith Grey features an ounce of her namesake's favorite liquor; Olivia Benson's *SVU* character is from Scotland, so Scotch swoops in for the kitten's version; and Benjamin Button's searing blue eyes inspired the color of his shot. Promise you'll never find another like any of them.

The Meredith Grey

1 OUNCE	REPOSADO TEQUILA
1/2 OUNCE	ORANGE JUICE
1/3 OUNCE	CHINOLA PASSION FRUIT LIQUEUR

For each shot, measure the ingredients into a shaker tin with ice and shake briefly to chill, then strain into a shot glass. Serve and cheers to your favorite furry friends, because you can't spell "meow" without me!

The Olivia Benson

1 OUNCE	SCOTCH OR RYE WHISKEY
1/2 OUNCE	FRESH LEMON JUICE
1/2 OUNCE	GRENADINE (PAGE 28)

The Benjamin Button

| 1 OUNCE | VODKA |
| 1 OUNCE | BLUE CURAÇAO |

And you can't spell "cats" without TS.

TAYLOR SPEAKS

"There was a point that I got to as a writer who only wrote very diaristic songs that I felt it was unsustainable for my future moving forward. So what I felt after we put out 'Folklore' was like, 'Oh wow, people are into this too, this thing that feels really good for my life and feels really good for my creativity . . . it feels good for them too?'"

—VARIETY, 2020

Folklore & Evermore

(2020)

During the coronavirus pandemic shutdown, Taylor's creative writing skyrocketed to a new level with *Folklore* and *Evermore*, which were released 140 days apart. As a result, we got something beautiful to help us get through a dark time. Both albums, which were produced and co-written with The National's Aaron Dressner, key into indie-folk vibes with introspective themes of melancholy, grief, and the deep emotional complexities of past relationships. Compared to her other albums, these two are particularly interesting, as she blurs the lines between fiction and autobiography with the backstories of each song. In line with the cottagecore vibes of this era, the recipes in this chapter stretch from contemplative old-fashioneds, like Peter Losing Wendy (page 122) and Only Seventeen (page 133), to a few sparkling ditties that star extra-complex flavor characters, like the Crestfallen Cure (page 137).

★ *As surprise albums,* Folklore *and* Evermore *bucked the traditional music–industry model of having intense marketing cycles leading up to the releases; this daring move proved how Tay continues to push the envelope with everything she does.*

★ Evermore *broke a Guinness World Record for the shortest gap between two number one albums on the Billboard 200; eight tracks from* Folklore *were still charting when* Evermore *came out, meaning she held 22 of the top 50 positions at the same time.*

★ *She received an honorary doctorate of fine arts degree from NYU during this time.*

TRACK "Cardigan"

DRINK *A cinnamon-
and smoke-laced
old-fashioned
for lingering over
memories of the past*

Peter Losing Wendy

Featuring aged tequila instead of whiskey, this old-fashioned is a nuanced companion for thinking back on how you kissed in cars and downtown bars and that's all you needed at the time. Whispers of smoky mezcal and mellow orange bitters unite in harmony, while cinnamon and chipotle-cacao bitters add a sting of heat to the memory. Like a worn-out old cardigan that still bears traces of love lost many years later, the finish lasts as long as a tattoo kiss.

1-1/2 OUNCES AÑEJO TEQUILA

1/2 OUNCE MEZCAL (PREFERABLY
DEL MAGUEY VIDA)

1/4 OUNCE CINNAMON SYRUP
(PAGE 27)

1 DASH ORANGE BITTERS
(PREFERABLY SCRAPPY'S)

1 DASH BITTERCUBE CHIPOTLE-
CACAO BITTERS

ORANGE PEEL,
FOR GARNISH

In a mixing glass, combine the two types of bitters, cinnamon syrup, mezcal, and tequila together with ice. Stir to chill. Strain into a double old-fashioned glass over one large ice cube. Flame the orange peel over the top of the glass, so the caramelized oils land on the surface of the drink. Discard the peel. Serve dancin' in your Levi's, drunk under a streetlight.

Holiday House

With perky pineapple and decadent orange liqueur, this extra-fruity mimosa-like cocktail is still tasteful, if a little loud. Made for mad women and their maddest legacies, it's an invigorating brunch drink—just what the doctor ordered for the morning after filling the pool with Champagne and swimming with the big names. In short, it's a marvelous drink for a marvelous time. Best served with homemade Pop-Tarts and cinnamon rolls.

1-1/2 OUNCES PINEAPPLE JUICE

1/2 OUNCE ORANGE LIQUEUR
(PREFERABLY
FERRAND DRY CURAÇAO)

1 DASH ORANGE BITTERS
(PREFERABLY
SCRAPPY'S)

4 TO 5 OUNCES CHAMPAGNE OR
SPARKLING WINE

LEMON TWIST,
FOR GARNISH

In an old-fashioned glass, combine the Champagne or sparkling wine with the orange bitters, orange liqueur, and pineapple juice. Add crushed ice and stir briefly to mingle all of the ingredients. Garnish by placing the lemon twist on the edge of the glass. Serve to your B*tch Pack friends from the city.

To Rebekah, Betty, Inez, James, Augustine, and the lives we all created around them

Insult to Injury

In one of her album voice memos for *Folklore,* Swift explains how "Exile" is about the way a series of miscommunications led to the demise of a relationship. "Even after they've broken up, they're still not hearing each other," she says of the end of the track where both parties are seemingly talking over one another, still not landing on the same page. When you didn't see it coming and can't turn things around, this apple-brandy Manhattan walks a thin line between bitter and sweet, offering a small respite from the anguish of losing your homeland.

3/4 OUNCE COGNAC
(OR IRISH WHISKEY OR
JAPANESE WHISKY)

3/4 OUNCE APPLE BRANDY

1-1/2 OUNCES SWEET VERMOUTH

2 DASHES ANGOSTURA BITTERS

ORANGE PEEL,
FOR GARNISH

LUXARDO MARASCHINO
CHERRY, FOR GARNISH

In a mixing glass three-quarters full of ice, combine the Angostura bitters with the sweet vermouth, apple brandy, and Cognac (or whiskey, if using). Stir and strain into a Nick and Nora glass. Squeeze the orange peel over the top of the drink to express the oils, and discard the peel. Plop a cherry into the glass or skewer it on a cocktail pick and rest it across the top. Serve and leave out the side door.

Stolen Lullaby

When all that's left are curses and tears, this cocktail, with its icy grip of gin, absinthe, and mint liqueur, will help lift the spirits. Thanks to the way lemon, lavender, and cocoa weave into the mix with grace, it's like a soft lullaby for when you can't sleep at night. Watch the tears run down the sides of the glass as you sip, ricocheting off the cocktail as it drains.

2 OUNCES GIN

3/4 OUNCE FRESH LEMON JUICE

1/2 OUNCE LAVENDER SYRUP (PAGE 28)

1/4 OUNCE CRÈME DE MENTHE

1 DASH ANGOSTURA COCOA BITTERS

1 TO 2 OUNCES ABSINTHE, TO RINSE THE GLASS

LEMON PEEL

2 FRESH LAVENDER SPRIGS, FOR GARNISH (OPTIONAL)

Prepare an old-fashioned glass: Fill it with crushed ice, add the absinthe, and stir until absinthe coats the interior of the glass. Set aside while you make the cocktail. In a shaker tin, combine the Angostura cocoa bitters, crème de menthe, lavender syrup, lemon juice, and gin with ice and shake to chill. Pour the crushed ice and absinthe out of the old-fashioned glass (into the sink), angling the glass as you do this so the absinthe continues to coat the interior of the glass on its way out. Refill the glass with crushed ice and strain the prepared cocktail into the ice. Squeeze the lemon peel over the top of the drink to express the oils and discard the peel. Add the fresh lavender sprigs (if using). Serve when you don't have it in yourself to go with grace.

FROM THE VAULT: *Typically low-proof, crème de menthe is a mint liqueur that brings a cooling quality to drinks. Sometimes it comes in neon green colors, but not always. Menthe-Pastille from Giffard is a spectacular choice for the cocktails in this book; it's made with peppermint essential oil instead of artificial flavorings (it's also clear—no fake colors), so its personality is searingly bright and fresh.*

Mine to Lose

As August slips away like a bottle of wine, this spin on the New York sour takes the classic cocktail into a slightly more sentimental direction. To change it for the better, a sun-soaked mix of whiskey and lemon sets a summery baseline for the brooding tannins and spice of black tea and Bénédictine. A red wine float laces the cocktail with subtle notes of red berries—use a good weeknight red like Cabernet Sauvignon, Syrah, or Malbec and you'll never need anything more. Cancel your plans, take a sip, and get lost in the memory.

2 OUNCES	WHISKEY (PREFERABLY IRISH WHISKEY)
1/4 OUNCE	BÉNÉDICTINE
1/2 OUNCE	BLACK TEA SYRUP (PAGE 26)
3/4 OUNCE	FRESH LEMON JUICE
1/2 OUNCE	DRY RED WINE, TO FLOAT
	LEMON PEEL

In a shaker tin, combine the lemon juice with the black tea syrup, Bénédictine, and whiskey. Add ice and shake to chill. Strain into a double old-fashioned glass over one large ice cube. To float the red wine on top, measure the wine into a jigger, place a barspoon upside down over the ice cube, then drizzle the wine over the back of the barspoon so it trickles slowly onto the ice. Squeeze the lemon peel over the top of the drink to express the oils, and discard the peel. Serve and meet me behind the mall.

TAYLOR SPEAKS

"I love writing songs because I love preserving memories, like putting a picture frame around a feeling you once had. I like to use nostalgia as inspiration when I'm writing songs for the same reason I like to take photographs. I like to be able to remember the extremely good and extremely bad times." —ELLE, 2019

Only Seventeen

When poor James realizes what he's lost by betraying Betty in the third chapter of the *Folklore* love triangle, it's hard to not feel bad for him. In the best love stories, apologies come with flowers, so for this cocktail, elderflower liqueur gently sweetens the smoky Scotch, a representation of the depths of James's remorse. The worst thing he ever did was what he did to her, but the worst thing you can do is skip this drink.

2 OUNCES SCOTCH

1/2 OUNCE ELDERFLOWER LIQUEUR

1/4 OUNCE DEMERARA SYRUP
(PAGE 25)

1 OR 2 DASHES ANGOSTURA BITTERS

LEMON PEEL,
FOR GARNISH

YELLOW EDIBLE
FLOWERS, FOR GARNISH

In a mixing glass, combine the Angostura bitters, demerara syrup, elderflower liqueur, and Scotch. Add ice and stir to chill, then strain into a double old-fashioned glass over a single large ice cube. Squeeze the lemon peel over the top of the drink to express the oils, and place the peel in the glass as a garnish, along with the edible flowers. Serve and hope for that kiss on the porch.

YOUR (N/A) VERSION: *James probably wouldn't make any assumptions if you wanted to make a booze-less version of this old-fashioned. Giffard makes a stunning spirit-free elderflower liqueur you can tie together with a good-quality whiskey sub, like Spiritless Kentucky 74 or Cut Above Spirits zero-proof whiskey. When synced up with All The Bitter aromatic bitters, they make a drink worth dreaming about all summer long.*

Spell Caster

Taylor says that, to her, the song "Willow" sounds like "casting a spell to make somebody fall in love with you." With enchanting green Chartreuse, sweet-spicy bitters, and aged tequila, this cocktail conjures the same vibes. Its moody, opulent flavors are a special breed of love magic, like a mythical thing. Wait for the signal—it's best consumed after dark.

1-1/2 OUNCES REPOSADO TEQUILA

1 OUNCE SWEET VERMOUTH

3/4 OUNCE GREEN CHARTREUSE

2 DASHES BITTERCUBE CHIPOTLE-CACAO BITTERS

LUXARDO MARASCHINO CHERRY, FOR GARNISH

LEMON PEEL

In a mixing glass, combine the chipotle-cacao bitters, green Chartreuse, sweet vermouth, and tequila. Add ice and stir to chill. (This is a very boozy cocktail, so stir for much longer than you would normally stir.) Strain into a chilled Nick and Nora glass. Squeeze the lemon peel over the top of the drink to express the oils, and discard the peel. To garnish, skewer the Luxardo cherry on a cocktail pick and rest it across the top of the glass. Serve and feel life bend right to your wind.

Crestfallen Cure

A sweet remedy for a haunting tale of unrequited love, this cocktail with a Midas touch sparkles with bright lemon juice and Champagne. A little Lillet Blanc, a Taylor fave, joins the glass to sweeten it up and welcome a supple floral note to the mix. She mentions Dom Pérignon in the song, but you can use your favorite sparkling wine and it will still taste delicious.

2 OUNCES	VODKA
3/4 OUNCE	LILLET BLANC
3/4 OUNCE	FRESH LEMON JUICE
1/2 OUNCE	SIMPLE SYRUP (PAGE 25)
4 OUNCES	CHAMPAGNE OR SPARKLING WINE
	LEMON PEEL, FOR GARNISH

Pour the Champagne or sparkling wine into a flute or a vintage cocktail glass. Set aside. Combine the simple syrup, lemon juice, Lillet Blanc, and vodka in a shaker tin with ice. Shake to chill, then strain into the Champagne. Squeeze the lemon peel over the top of the drink to express the oils. You can put the peel in the glass if it looks pretty, or discard it. Serve and sit in the hurt.

FROM THE VAULT: *For a pretty pink version of this drink, Lillet makes a rosé version of its famous aperitif. It pairs swimmingly with a good sparkling rosé wine.*

 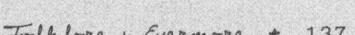

Amber Skies

Phone flashlights up! It's time to send sparkling lights to all of the strong women who came before us. "Marjorie" was written as an ode to Taylor's grandmother, an opera singer who inspired Tay to pursue a career in music. In homage to this tender relationship, this warm hot toddy is as comforting as hearing a loved one sing backup on your favorite track. Taylor has talked about how her grandmother had a fondness for good whiskey, and this hot toddy features a generous slug of bourbon for her enduring wisdom, a little cinnamon for her kind cleverness, and a splash of port as a toast to her legacy.

1-1/2 OUNCES BOURBON

1/2 OUNCE TAWNY PORT

1/2 OUNCE CINNAMON SYRUP
(PAGE 27)

1 DASH ANGOSTURA BITTERS

5 OUNCES BOILING WATER

ORANGE PEEL,
FOR GARNISH

In a coffee mug or large teacup, add the boiling water. Set aside. In a mixing glass, combine the Angostura bitters, cinnamon syrup, port, and bourbon. Stir briefly to combine the ingredients, then strain into the mug with the hot water. Squeeze the orange peel over the top of the drink to express the oils, and place the peel in the mug as a garnish. Serve and remember: Never be so polite, you forget your power, and never wield such power, you forget to be polite.

TAYLOR SPEAKS

"I think of Midnights *as a complete concept album, with those 13 songs forming a full picture of the intensities of that mystifying, mad hour."*

—INSTAGRAM POST, 2022

Midnights

(2022)

Throughout the years, T-Swift would often talk about how her most creative ideas arrived in the middle of the night, when she'd put pen to paper to exorcise her deepest fears and anxieties—and to wax poetic about her hopes and dreams. *Midnights* is the culmination of those witching-hour sessions. During this time, as she changed her aesthetic to midnight blues, purples, sparkles, and jewel tones, she aptly described the record as "a sultry, sleepless '70s fever dream." From the first beats of "Lavender Haze," that vibe tracks! To ride the wave of this era in style, the cocktails in this chapter are a little more playful than in some others, with drinks like the YOYOKolada (page 149) serving as a matcha-flavored twist on the piña colada, and the Tactical Tonic (page 154) bringing colorful whimsy to the G&T canvas with its grapefruit ice cubes.

★ *In 2023, Taylor was named TIME's Person of the Year, appearing on the cover in a striking black leotard with her fur baby Benjamin Button draped around her shoulders.*

★ *The same year, she announced the Eras Tour, which would celebrate her entire discography by featuring shows lasting more than two hours, with upward of 40 songs over at least nine albums. Eras would take the world by storm, becoming the highest-grossing concert tour of all time.*

★ *Tay continued her collaboration with Jack Antonoff on this album—he co-wrote 11 of the 13 songs. She compiled a collection of seven extra songs that didn't make the cut for the first album and released them as "3am" tracks.*

Violet Love Spiral

Named after the phrase commonly used to describe being in love in the 1950s—Taylor first heard it on an episode of *Mad Men*—this song extends the metaphor to refer to the way people in the honeymoon phase of love want to do everything to stay inside their happy bubble. Like swimming in a shimmering purple-dyed pool or dancing in plumes of purple smoke, this cocktail feels as dreamy as blissful infatuation. Sip it and feel that lavender haze creepin' up.

2 OUNCES GIN

3/4 OUNCE FRESH LEMON JUICE

3/4 OUNCE LAVENDER SYRUP (PAGE 28)

1 DASH PEYCHAUD'S BITTERS

PURPLE EDIBLE GLITTER (OPTIONAL)

4 OUNCES CLUB SODA

LEMON PEEL, FOR GARNISH

FRESH LAVENDER SPRIGS, FOR GARNISH (OPTIONAL)

Add 4 or 5 ice cubes and the club soda to a Collins glass and set aside. In a shaker tin, combine the edible glitter (if using), Peychaud's bitters, lavender syrup, lemon juice, and gin. Add ice and shake to chill, then strain the cocktail into the prepared Collins glass. Squeeze the lemon peel over the top of the drink to express the oils, and place the peel and a few lavender sprigs (if using) in the glass to garnish. Serve and get it off your chest.

YOUR (N/A) VERSION: *There's never any shame in choosing a booze-free version of a cocktail when the occasion calls for it—you'll be damned if you do give a damn what people say. In this case, simply use an N/A gin in place of the regular spirit. This cocktail tastes great with Seedlip Garden 108, because it has a demure herbaceous quality that lets the lavender syrup shine, but you can experiment with other brands as the spirit moves. Just omit the Peychaud's bitters if you want a drink that is 100 percent alcohol-free. Talk your talk, and go viral!*

Scarlet Rust

It's as if Taylor puts on reverse-rose-colored glasses when reflecting on a troubled relationship in this song—instead of memories looking rosy, they're all brooding shades of maroon. Tequila sets a verdant tone for this cocktail, while crème de cassis splashes in at the end, leaving a memorable impression. Like the rust that grew between telephones, watch how the blackcurrant liqueur slowly bleeds into the crushed ice as it sinks to the bottom. Like a burgundy stain on a T-shirt, it's so scarlet, it's maroon.

2 OUNCES	BLANCO TEQUILA
3/4 OUNCE	FRESH LIME JUICE
1/2 OUNCE	SIMPLE SYRUP (PAGE 25)
1 DASH	ORANGE BITTERS (PREFERABLY SCRAPPY'S)
1/4 OUNCE	CRÈME DE CASSIS, TO FLOAT

In a shaker tin, combine the orange bitters, simple syrup, lime juice, and blanco tequila with ice and shake to chill. Strain into a Collins glass filled with crushed ice. Garnish by drizzling the crème de cassis over the ice. Feel the blood rush into your cheeks as you serve.

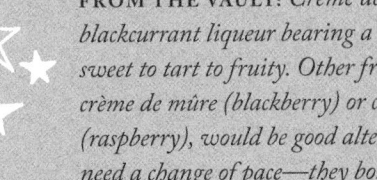

FROM THE VAULT: *Crème de cassis is a blackcurrant liqueur bearing a lovely balance of sweet to tart to fruity. Other fruit liqueurs, like crème de mûre (blackberry) or crème de framboise (raspberry), would be good alternatives when you need a change of pace—they both have a similarly boisterous fruit quality and a color just like the carnations you thought were roses (maroon).*

TRACK *"Anti-Hero"*   DRINK *It's tea. Hi.*
It's in this cocktail.
It's tea.

T-Swizzle's Tea Swizzle

When left to its own devices, rum is often looked at as an antihero in the spirits world. But at teatime, everybody agrees it can be one of the most flavorful of spirits when paired with the right ingredients. In this case, aged rum finds its place alongside sumptuous passion fruit liqueur—a flavor so bright it's like staring at the sun—and a subtle backbone of black tea. Mix one up when feelings of self-loathing need banishing. Taylor, you'll be fine!

2 OUNCES	AGED RUM
1/2 OUNCE	CHINOLA PASSION FRUIT LIQUEUR
3/4 OUNCE	FRESH LEMON JUICE
1/2 OUNCE	BLACK TEA SYRUP (PAGE 26)
1 DASH	ANGOSTURA BITTERS
	BOUQUET OF MINT, FOR GARNISH
	LEMON TWIST, FOR GARNISH

In a shaker tin, combine the Angostura bitters, black tea syrup, lemon juice, passion fruit liqueur, and aged rum with ice and shake to chill. Strain into an old-fashioned glass filled with crushed ice and garnish with the mint bouquet and a lemon twist, hanging over the side of the glass. Serve and be that monster on the hill.

YOYOKolada

Adulting is hard, especially when you realize that at the end of the day, you're on your own and you always have been. From sprinkler splashes to fireplace ashes, the journey of balancing youthful exuberance with self-made independence is like navigating the most choppy waters. But you've got no reason to be afraid—we've all been there. Play it cool with this piña colada that takes a turn into adulthood with the addition of matcha tea. (The matcha turns this cocktail a vibrant green hue—the perfect inspiration for the color of your next friendship bracelet.) The yin-yang of fruity fun flavors and grassy sophisticated ones just begs you to lean in. Take the moment and taste it!

2 OUNCES	WHITE RUM (PREFERABLY PLANTERAY 3 STAR)
1-1/2 OUNCES	PINEAPPLE JUICE
1-1/2 OUNCES	COCONUT CREAM (UNSWEETENED)
1/2 OUNCE	FRESH LIME JUICE
1/2 OUNCE	SIMPLE SYRUP (PAGE 25)
1 TEASPOON	MATCHA POWDER
5 CHUNKS	FROZEN PINEAPPLE
	FRESH PINEAPPLE SPEARS, FOR GARNISH

Add ½ cup of crushed ice to a blender, followed by the frozen pineapple chunks, matcha, simple syrup, lime juice, coconut cream, pineapple juice, and white rum, and blend until smooth. Strain into your favorite tropical mug. Serve, turn the page, burn the bridge, you've got no reason to be afraid.

YOUR (N/A) VERSION: *If you're in the mood to play it cool with the best of them, you can omit the rum, or use a zero-proof version, to make this drink booze-less.*

Sapphire Martini

No drink is better suited for a night on the town like a well-made martini. But like Taylor says, familiarity breeds contempt. So to spruce up the same-old-same-old, this version is bejeweled with a few shining upgrades. First, blanc vermouth brings an enchantingly sweet personality to the glass. Second, a bump of caviar on the side is the ultimate way to set the tone for dancing all night. Make it with an extra-luxe vodka, like Absolut Elyx, and it'll shine like only the penthouse of vodka martinis can. Put on your best shoes, hit the town, make the whole place shimmer!

2 OUNCES	VODKA
1 OUNCE	DOLIN BLANC VERMOUTH
3 DASHES	ORANGE BITTERS (PREFERABLY SCRAPPY'S)
1 TEASPOON	CAVIAR, TO BUMP
	LEMON PEEL

In a mixing glass with ice, combine the orange bitters, blanc vermouth, and vodka. Stir to chill, then strain into a martini glass. Garnish by expressing the oils of the lemon peel over the top of the drink. Discard the peel. Dollop that bump of caviar on the back of your hand and lick it off, then sip with diamonds in your eyes.

The Guy on the Chiefs

Fact: Taylor believes that sometimes karma isn't something horrible that comes back at you but something sweet and wonderful that boomerangs around if you've put that energy out into the universe. That's definitely been the case with her relationship with Travis Kelce from the Kansas City Chiefs football team. Together they are practically Mr. and Mrs. Americana. This song wasn't written about Kelce, because they didn't start dating until the album was already out, but their romance fits the concept so well that we're rolling with it. The recipe is inspired by the Grey Goose Honey Deuce, the cocktail Taylor and Travis were spied drinking with friends at the US Open in 2024. With honey syrup and muddled raspberries, it's a fresh update on the original.

2 OUNCES	VODKA
3/4 OUNCE	FRESH LEMON JUICE
3/4 OUNCE	HONEY SYRUP (PAGE 26)
7	RASPBERRIES
4 OUNCES	CLUB SODA
	LEMON PEEL, FOR GARNISH

Add 4 or 5 ice cubes and the club soda to your favorite football mug. In a shaker tin, muddle 6 of the raspberries, then add the honey syrup, lemon juice, and vodka. Add ice and shake to chill. Double-strain into the mug: Hold a fine-mesh strainer underneath the Hawthorne strainer as you strain.. Squeeze the lemon peel over the top of the drink to express the oils, then skewer the peel on a cocktail pick and add the remaining raspberry to the pick as garnish. Serve if you believe in a thing called love.

YOUR (N/A) VERSION: *To keep your side of the street clean, the alcohol-free version of this drink is sweet like honey, like a cat purring in your lap, like flexing like a godd*mn acrobat! The path to deliciousness is uncomplicated: Try Seedlip Grove 42 or Clean V—a vodka alternative from CleanCo with a lovely cinnamon flavor—in place of the vodka and feel the breeze in your hair on the weekend. Karma should always taste this good.*

Tactical Tonic

Make no mistake, it's so fun trying to unearth the mastermind schemes T-Swift infuses into her songs and marketing campaigns. So it's only fitting that this tall cooler is created with as many careful calculations as she puts into her craft. On paper, it looks like an audacious gin and tonic—and it starts out boozy AF—but like clockwork, the grapefruit ice cubes melt and the mix becomes bright, like a paloma-meets-G&T. None of this is accidental. As the drink changes with each sip, the stars align. It's so delicious, it should be criminal.

2 OUNCES GIN

1/4 OUNCE CAMPARI

3 TO 4 OUNCES TONIC WATER
(PREFERABLY
FEVER-TREE)

2 GRAPEFRUIT JUICE
ICE CUBES

GRAPEFRUIT WHEEL,
FOR GARNISH

A day before you want to make this cocktail, fill a silicone ice cube tray with grapefruit juice and freeze overnight.

To make the drink, grab a Collins glass and add ice cubes, alternating grapefruit ice and regular ice, until the glass is about three-quarters full. Add the tonic water, Campari, and gin. Give it a quick stir to integrate the ingredients, and garnish with a grapefruit wheel. Serve and checkmate.

TAYLOR SPEAKS

"This writer is of the firm belief that our tears become holy in the form of ink on a page. Once we have spoken our saddest story, we can be free of it. And then all that's left behind is the tortured poetry."

—INSTAGRAM POST, 2024

The Tortured Poets Department

(2024)

As her most fantastically dramatic project to date, *The Tortured Poets Department* is classic Taylor, with the rich lyricism from *Folklore, Evermore,* and *Midnights* brought to life by lush, almost cinematic soundscapes. With both Jack Antonoff and Aaron Dressner co-writing tracks, the vibe ranges from vivid radio bangers—see "Florida!!!" with Florence Welch from Florence and the Machine—to more moody ones like "Fortnight," performed with Post Malone. As the Queen herself says in the liner notes, "all's fair in love and poetry," so the cocktails in this final chapter reflect the same high/low dynamic. For "Florida!!!", an ultimately refreshing Floridita daiquiri (page 162). For "Fortnight," a potent stirred requiem for a short-lived affair, with smoke, cherries, and chocolate (page 158). And the book wraps with a boozy drink that punches with the same power as Tay: The Best of Me (page 169).

★ *Only a few hours after the initial release, Taylor announced that* The Tortured Poets Department *was, in fact, a secret double album: The anthology brings the total track list to 31 songs.*

★ *In the months following the release of the album, critical reviews were divided, with some calling it messy and disjointed, others saying she played it too safe, and some claiming it's spectacular storytelling.*

★ *A 2024 survey stated that 1 in 5 viewers rooted for the Kansas City Chiefs during the Super Bowl strictly due to Taylor's relationship with Travis Kelce.*

Miracle Move-On Drug

In homage to the compelling on-screen magic between the personas Tay and costar Post Malone play in the "Fortnight" music video, this cocktail features a hefty dose of sweet vermouth (for its opulent cherry and dried rosemary flavors) and chocolate liqueur (to pump up the sweetness). A tiny measure of mezcal creates a finish that hangs on long after the moment has passed, reminding us how a fortnight can be too short a time to make romance stick yet long enough to leave a lasting impression. The effects of the cocktail, unfortunately, are temporary.

1/2 OUNCE MEZCAL (PREFERABLY DEL MAGUEY VIDA)

1-1/2 OUNCES SWEET VERMOUTH

1 BARSPOON LUXARDO MARASCHINO LIQUEUR

1 BARSPOON CRÈME DE CACAO

1 DASH ANGOSTURA COCOA BITTERS

LUXARDO MARASCHINO CHERRY, FOR GARNISH

In a mixing glass, combine the Angostura cocoa bitters with the crème de cacao, maraschino liqueur, sweet vermouth, and mezcal. Add ice and stir to chill, then strain into a Nick and Nora glass. Garnish with the maraschino cherry. Serve and move to Florida, buy the car you want.

Stormy Soliloquy

Loving someone who others don't approve of conjures a complex brew of feelings. Staying confident and steadfast while navigating the pain is tough, and Taylor's determination to follow her heart and embrace the chaos and revelry cuts through all the noise. Forget the Sarahs and Hannahs, this take on the Dark 'n Stormy is for times that call for wild joy and self-preservation. It has the ferocious spice of ginger at the forefront, bolstered by high-proof rum and a backup chorus of bitters.

1-1/2 OUNCES	OVERPROOF AGED RUM (PREFERABLY PLANTERAY OFTD)
3/4 OUNCE	GINGER LIQUEUR
3/4 OUNCE	FRESH LIME JUICE
1/4 OUNCE	DEMERARA SYRUP (PAGE 25)
1 DASH	ANGOSTURA BITTERS
1/2 OUNCE	BLACKSTRAP RUM, TO FLOAT
	LIME WHEEL, FOR GARNISH

In a shaker tin with ice, combine the Angostura bitters, demerara syrup, lime juice, ginger liqueur, and overproof aged rum. Shake to chill and strain into a Collins glass over crushed ice. Place a barspoon upside down over the ice, then drizzle the blackstrap rum over the spoon's back to float. Perch the lime wheel on the rim to garnish. Serve with wild joy.

YOUR (N/A) VERSION: *No need to clutch your pearls if a zero-proof version of this drink is on deck instead of its boozy counterpart. Tenneyson makes an alcohol-free black ginger liqueur that adds a robust spice quality to the drink, and for the alcohol-free rum substitute, Three Spirit Nightcap is a nice choice to use thanks to its bouquet of maple, vanilla, and ginger notes. All The Bitter's aromatic bitters swing in with a new perspective on the traditional Ango, and—you should see your faces—it's that easy.*

TAYLOR SPEAKS

"The writing I love the most places you into that story, that room, that rain-soaked kiss. You can smell the air, hear the sounds, and feel your heart race as the character's does."
—ELLE, 2019

Flo! Florida! Floridita!

For when you need to beat the heat and bury your regrets, the Floridita can be one hell of a drug. The 1930s-era daiquiri variation hails from Florida's southern neighbor Havana, where the Cuban cantineros whip up batches by the blenderful. This snappy rum drink has only a tiny bit of maraschino liqueur, but its floral cherry note blossoms the way the chorus in this song does, making the cocktail as memorable as Florence Welch's force-of-nature guest appearance in the song.

2 OUNCES	WHITE RUM (PREFERABLY PLANTERAY 3 STAR)
3/4 OUNCE	FRESH LIME JUICE
1/4 OUNCE	LUXARDO MARASCHINO LIQUEUR
1 OUNCE	SIMPLE SYRUP (PAGE 25)
	EDIBLE FLOWER, FOR GARNISH

Add the liquid ingredients to the jar of a blender: first the simple syrup, then the maraschino liqueur, lime juice, and white rum. Add 1 cup of crushed ice and blend until smooth, then pour into a martini glass. Garnish with an edible flower. Drink it and dare it to wash you away.

French Blondie

It's easy to underestimate drinks like the French Blonde—one of Taylor's favorites—because it looks floral and flirty and pretty at first sight but has a fiery punch of booze at its core. One sip and you'll levitate down the street. Strong-willed, confident, poised for the attack: This version of the cocktail has it all. Sounds a lot like everyone's favorite songstress, no? Who's afraid of Blondie? Well, she's so fierce, maybe we all should be.

1 OUNCE GIN (PREFERABLY FORD'S)

2 OUNCES LILLET BLANC

1/2 OUNCE ELDERFLOWER LIQUEUR

2 OUNCES GRAPEFRUIT JUICE

1/4 OUNCE SIMPLE SYRUP (PAGE 25)

2 DASHES GRAPEFRUIT BITTERS

GRAPEFRUIT TWIST, FOR GARNISH

In a shaker tin, combine the grapefruit bitters, simple syrup, grapefruit juice, elderflower liqueur, Lillet Blanc, and gin. Add ice and shake to chill, then strain into a coupe glass. Garnish with the grapefruit twist. Serve and crash the party like a record scratch.

TAYLOR SPEAKS

"Oh, God—I wouldn't give myself any advice. I would have done everything exactly the same way. Because even the really tough things I've gone through taught me things that I never would have learned any other way. I really appreciate my experience, the ups and downs. And maybe that seems ridiculously Zen, but . . . I've got my friends, who like me for the right reasons. I've got my family. I've got my boyfriend. I've got my fans. I've got my cats."
—BILLBOARD, 2015

Sequined Stars and Silhouettes

With a drink this delicious in hand, you won't have to pretend it's your birthday every day, you'll just feel like it is. Tapping into the feeling that comes with hitting all the right marks despite the misery that bubbles under the surface, this lowball is bright and refreshing, the sharp sherry and bracing tonic softened by the effortless cool of cucumber. When you've given something your all, even when you're not really in the mood to do it, you deserve to treat yourself, so let's do this. One, two, three: lights, camera, b*tch, smile.

<u>2 OUNCES</u> FINO SHERRY (PREFERABLY LUSTAU)

<u>2</u> SLICES CUCUMBER, QUARTERED

<u>4 TO 5 OUNCES</u> TONIC WATER (PREFERABLY FEVER-TREE)

CUCUMBER WHEEL, FOR GARNISH

Add one large ice cube and the tonic water to a double old-fashioned glass; set aside. In a shaker tin, muddle the cucumber slices, then add the sherry and ice; shake to chill. Double-strain the cocktail into the prepared glass: Hold a fine-mesh strainer underneath the Hawthorne strainer as you strain. Garnish with the cucumber wheel. Serve and try to come for my job.

YOUR (N/A) VERSION: *Alcohol-free sherries aren't really a thing yet as far as we know, but you could use an N/A gin in this recipe and it'll feel just as uplifting. Seedlip Garden 108 has a soft-spoken botanical profile that matches the frequency of the cucumber so well it's almost grinning like it's winning.*

The Best of Me

Three pitch-black ingredients come together in tribute to "The Black Dog," an elegy to longing, confusion, and a dark nostalgia that won't go away without a fight. Consider it a more brooding take on the classic espresso martini, as two types of coffee intertwine with the magical intensity of Fernet-Branca. Sell the house, set fire to your clothes, hire a priest to exorcise those demons—this dark beauty captures it all.

1 OUNCE COLD-BREW COFFEE CONCENTRATE

1 OUNCE FERNET-BRANCA

1 OUNCE COFFEE LIQUEUR

ORANGE PEEL

3 COFFEE BEANS, FOR GARNISH

Combine the coffee liqueur, Fernet, and cold-brew coffee concentrate in a shaker tin with ice, and shake to chill. Strain into a martini glass. Squeeze the orange peel over the top of the drink to express the oils, and discard the peel. Drop in the coffee beans. Serve when you've got no choice but to move through the world heartbroken, longings unspoken.

FROM THE VAULT: *Coffee lovers know that old habits die screaming, but if you're trying to steer clear of caffeine, you can use decaf cold-brew concentrate in this drink—the same deliciousness without the extra buzz. Ditto for the Fernet: If amaro is not your thing, you can use vodka or blanco tequila in its place for a less bitter version.*

I remember it.

THANK
YOU

FROM ALISON GREY:

First and foremost, to the incomparable **JENN SIT:** Thank you for thinking of me for this project. I am so grateful for our collaborations, and especially the ones that create space for so much unbridled joy. My agent, **KIM WITHERSPOON:** I appreciate you going to bat for me with the details, both large and small! You're the best. **IAN DINGMAN, STEPHANIE HUNTWORK,** and **KELLY PULEIO** (and your design and photo teams), y'all blew this one out of the water and I will forever be in awe of your mad skills. Thanks to the rest of the Clarkson Potter production team as well, including **TERRY DEAL, JESSICA HEIM,** and **CLANCY DRAKE.**

MELANIE, my number one Swiftie, I couldn't have done this without your expertise and encouragement. **TOBY,** our ongoing writing collaborations have made me the "bartender" I am today; I hope you delight in seeing your influence sprinkled throughout these recipes. **ZACH,** you are forever the best partner, and in this case especially so for enduring the long nights of recipe development, which were accompanied by an endless loop of the Eras Pour soundtrack blasting in the background. I promise, no more "me-hee-heeeees" at eleven p.m. while you're trying to watch football. Also, thanks to **MY PARENTS** for the occasional "how does this drink taste" feedback.

Thanks to teams at **RACHEL HARRISON COMMUNICATIONS** and **SAVONA COMMUNICATIONS** for helping facilitate samples for recipe testing, and to the alcohol-free brands who also supported this book by sending samples to play with: Your work makes the world a more inclusive and delicious place for the folks who are not drinking booze (for whatever reason), which is gold. The recipes within these pages are more delicious for it!

Finally, to **TAYLOR SWIFT,** for lighting up the world with everything she does, and to her **SWIFTIES** everywhere: This book is for y'all!

FROM KELLY PULEIO, PHOTOGRAPHER:

A huge thank-you to the amazing photo team—**KAEJA, TREVIN, KATJA, ALEX,** and **TAMARA**—for going above and beyond at every step of this project. **KAEJA,** your creativity, partnership, and endless energy brought our vision to life in the most beautiful ways. I'm so grateful for you! **TREVIN,** cocktail master, you have three seconds! Thank you for always delivering perfection, no matter the ask. **KATJA,** the master of light, you read my mind and make everything even more beautiful. Thank you for being exactly who you are, I am forever grateful. **ALEX,** you are pure light. Thank you for every single thing you do and for bringing such warmth to the set. **TAMARA,** my love, you make spreadsheets a work of art. Thank you for your tireless support and everything you do to keep us all running smoothly. **WOODY ECKENRODE** and **LEAH CRONIN,** for being the most dedicated and thoughtful Swiftie consultants. **WOODY,** thank you for the inspiration and painting the sweetest bar napkins featuring all our pups. **LEAH,** thank you for the sixty-four-page color-coded deck and lending us your vast collection of friendship bracelets. **JEN WALTERS,** for being the most natural and down-for-anything hand model! You're magic! **KENZIE TAYLOR,** for a perfect handmade mini, bedazzled guitar. **KAEJA'S AUNT TESS,** for passing down her beloved vintage collection. I'm truly grateful for each of you!

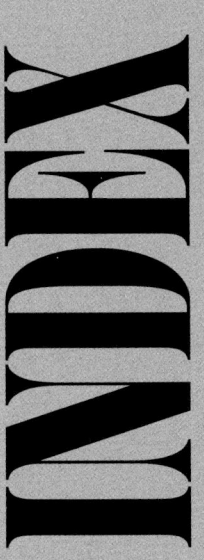

INDEX

NOTE: PAGE REFERENCES IN *ITALICS* INDICATE PHOTOGRAPHS.

CLARKSON POTTER/PUBLISHERS
AN IMPRINT OF THE CROWN
PUBLISHING GROUP
A DIVISION OF PENGUIN RANDOM HOUSE LLC
1745 BROADWAY, NEW YORK, NY 10019
CLARKSONPOTTER.COM
PENGUINRANDOMHOUSE.COM

LIBRARY OF CONGRESS CATALOGING-IN-
PUBLICATION DATA.
LC RECORD AVAILABLE AT HTTPS://LCCN.
LOC.GOV/2024055507
LC EBOOK RECORD AVAILABLE AT HTTPS://
LCCN.LOC.GOV/2024055508

ISBN 979-8-217-03441-3
EBOOK ISBN 979-8-217-03442-0

PHOTOGRAPHY: KELLY PULEIO
PHOTO ART DIRECTION: KELLY PULEIO +
KAEJA KORTY
PHOTO PRODUCER: TAMARA COSTA
PHOTO ASSISTANT + LIGHTING: KATJA
BRESCH
COCKTAIL STYLING: TREVIN HUTCHINS
PROP STYLIST: KAEJA KORTY
PROP ASSISTANT: ALEX CRAVEN
TALENT: JEN HARDY

EDITOR: JENNIFER SIT
EDITORIAL ASSISTANT: ELAINE HENNIG
DESIGNER + ILLUSTRATOR: IAN DINGMAN
ART DIRECTORS: STEPHANIE HUNTWORK +
IAN DINGMAN
PRODUCTION DESIGNER: CHRISTINA SELF
PRODUCTION EDITOR: TERRY DEAL
PRODUCTION: JESSICA HEIM
COMPOSITORS: MERRI ANN MORRELL +
HANNAH HUNT
COPY EDITOR: CLANCY DRAKE
PROOFREADER: AMELIA IUVINO +
RACHEL MARKOWITZ
INDEXER: THÉRÈSE SHERE
PUBLICIST: LAUREN CHUNG
MARKETER: STEPHANIE DAVIS

MANUFACTURED IN THE USA

2nd Printing

FIRST EDITION

THE AUTHORIZED REPRESENTATIVE IN THE EU
FOR PRODUCT SAFETY AND COMPLIANCE IS
PENGUIN RANDOM HOUSE IRELAND, MORRISON
CHAMBERS, 32 NASSAU STREET, DUBLIN D02
YH68, IRELAND, HTTPS://EU-CONTACT.
PENGUIN.IE.